Twentieth-Century American Writers

Other Books in the History Makers Series:

Twentieth-Century American Writers

By Elizabeth Meehan

Lucent Books
P.O. Box 289011, San Diego, CA 92198-9011

On Cover: Ernest Hemingway (center), James Baldwin (top right), John Steinbeck (bottom right), Toni Morrison (bottom left), William Faulkner (top left).

Library of Congress Cataloging-in-Publication Data

Meehan, Elizabeth.
    Twentieth-century American writers / by Elizabeth Meehan.
        p. cm. — (History makers)
    Includes bibliographical references and index.
    Summary: Profiles the lives and work of the following twentieth-century American writers: John Steinbeck, Ernest Hemingway, William Faulkner, James Baldwin, Flannery O'Connor, and Toni Morrison.
    ISBN 1-56006-671-7 (alk. paper)
    1. American literature—20th century—History and criticism—Juvenile literature. 2. Authors, American—20th century—Biography—Juvenile literature. [1. American literature—20th century—History and criticism. 2. Authors, American.] I. Title. II. Series.
    PS221 .M397 2000
    810.9'005—dc21

                                                    99-050796

Printed in the U.S.A.

CONTENTS

FOREWORD

The literary form most often referred to as "multiple biography" was perfected in the first century A.D. by Plutarch, a perceptive and talented moralist and historian who hailed from the small town of Chaeronea in central Greece. His most famous work, *Parallel Lives*, consists of a long series of biographies of noteworthy ancient Greek and Roman statesmen and military leaders. Frequently, Plutarch compares a famous Greek to a famous Roman, pointing out similarities in personality and achievements. These expertly constructed and very readable tracts provided later historians and others, including playwrights like Shakespeare, with priceless information about prominent ancient personages and also inspired new generations of writers to tackle the multiple biography genre.

The Lucent History Makers series proudly carries on the venerable tradition handed down from Plutarch. Each volume in the series consists of a set of five to eight biographies of important and influential historical figures who were linked together by a common factor. In *Rulers of Ancient Rome*, for example, all the figures were generals, consuls, or emperors of either the Roman Republic or Empire; while the subjects of *Fighters Against American Slavery*, though they lived in different places and times, all shared the same goal, namely the eradication of human servitude. Mindful that politicians and military leaders are not (and never have been) the only people who shape the course of history, the editors of the series have also included representatives from a wide range of endeavors, including scientists, artists, writers, philosophers, religious leaders, and sports figures.

Each book is intended to give a range of figures—some well known, others less known; some who made a great impact on history, others who made only a small impact. For instance, by making Columbus's initial voyage possible, Spain's Queen Isabella I, featured in *Women Leaders of Nations*, helped to open up the New World to exploration and exploitation by the European powers. Unarguably, therefore, she made a major contribution to a series of events that had momentous consequences for the entire world. By contrast, Catherine II, the eighteenth-century Russian queen, and Golda Meir, the modern Israeli prime minister, did not play roles of global impact; however, their policies and actions significantly influenced the historical development of both their own countries and their regional neighbors. Regardless of their relative importance in the greater historical scheme, all of the figures chronicled in the History Makers series made contributions to posterity; and their public achievements, as well as what is known about their private lives, are presented and evaluated in light of the most recent scholarship.

In addition, each volume in the series is documented and substantiated by a wide array of primary and secondary source quotations. The primary source quotes enliven the text by presenting eyewitness views of the times and culture in which each history maker lived; while the secondary source quotes, taken from the works of respected modern scholars, offer expert elaboration and/or critical commentary. Each quote is footnoted, demonstrating to the reader exactly where biographers find their information. The footnotes also provide the reader with the means of conducting additional research. Finally, to further guide and illuminate readers, each volume in the series features photographs, two bibliographies, and a comprehensive index.

The History Makers series provides both students engaged in research and more casual readers with informative, enlightening, and entertaining overviews of individuals from a variety of circumstances, professions, and backgrounds. No doubt all of them, whether loved or hated, benevolent or cruel, constructive or destructive, will remain endlessly fascinating to each new generation seeking to identify the forces that shaped their world.

Chroniclers of American Society

Throughout human history, every society in every age has relied on its writers to speak of events, both momentous and minor. Taken together, the literature of a given society tells of its members' hopes, fears, tribulations, and aspirations. This is no less true of America's writers, although in a society as diverse as the United States in the twentieth century, no one author can claim to speak for Americans as a whole. Yet, each of the writers profiled here speaks profoundly and eloquently of some aspect of the American experience.

John Steinbeck, for example, fixed in the minds of his countrymen unforgettable images of the poor and dispossessed. In novels such as *Cannery Row*, *The Pearl*, and, most notably, *The Grapes of Wrath*, Steinbeck depicted the struggles of those society seemed to have forgotten.

Ernest Hemingway created characters who embodied qualities that many thought of as quintessentially American, such as honesty, courage, and endurance. Through prose that was uniquely lean and direct, Hemingway gave the world images that were startling in their clarity. Few can forget, for example, the image in *For Whom the Bell Tolls* of a lone American volunteer, Robert Jordan, facing death alone during the Spanish Civil War.

William Faulkner was as subtle as Hemingway was direct. Faulkner grew up watching his fellow southerners battle the ghosts of a troubled past. He took the experiences of members of his own family and those of the people he came in contact with on a daily basis to create his own society. Unforgettable for both its lazy sensuality and its unspeakable brutality, the society known as Yoknapatawpha County, Mississippi, embodied the hopes and fears of an entire region of America.

James Baldwin dealt with some of the same ghosts as Faulkner, but from a different perspective. Whereas Faulkner wrote about a society that had destroyed itself by clinging stubbornly to traditions dating back to slavery times, Baldwin wrote as a member of the group the South had enslaved. Baldwin's mission was to speak clearly of what it was like to be African American in a society that had little use for its black members. Openly gay at a time when most gays carefully hid their sexual orientation, Baldwin spoke too of what it meant to be homosexual.

Flannery O'Connor, like her fellow southerner William Faulkner, drew from among the people she knew to create her characters. Unlike Faulkner's characters, who often seem beyond redemption, O'Connor's characters appear headed for redemption in spite of themselves.

Toni Morrison, currently at the height of her creative powers, uses fabulous imagery to depict the struggles of African Americans to make sense not just of their past but also of their present. Her novels represent an ongoing effort to develop her narrative voice, which calls on all who read them to pay attention to the past, present, and future.

Although few of these authors met with immediate success, each was eventually recognized as having made a significant contribution to American literature. While these writers tell of the struggles of people to make their way in the world, their personal lives make fascinating reading and in some cases illuminate their works.

CHAPTER 1

A New Literature for a New Society

As the nineteenth century turned into the twentieth, enormous changes were at work in American society. No longer would it be possible to think of America as a nation largely built by people whose native tongue was English. Although America had always accepted immigrants, those who arrived in the nation's ports and settled in its cities came from increasingly diverse cultures. In addition to Scandinavians and other western Europeans, immigrants came from eastern Europe and Asia and across America's southern border as well. In the first decades of the new century, millions of immigrants arrived. As an American historian notes, these new immigrants were a diverse lot: "As in the 1890s, the immigrant stream flowed primarily from southern and eastern Europe, but 200,000 Japanese, 40,000 Chinese, and thousands of Mexicans joined them."[1]

In addition to the new arrivals from abroad, America's cities became home to what might be thought of as domestic immigrants: Changes in the farm economy meant that a steady stream of people left their rural homes to make new lives in cities such as New York, Detroit, and Chicago. These new city dwellers were joined by legions of African Americans who, like their white counterparts, were searching for steady jobs that offered the hope for a better life in the cities of the American North.

If the new immigrants thought life would be easy, however, they were sadly mistaken. Conditions in American cities could be appalling. One historian says of America's cities during the early twentieth century, "Death rates in the immigrant wards [neighborhoods] reached twice the national average, reflecting shockingly bad conditions."[2] These immigrants' attempts to integrate into American society as a whole would eventually be reflected in American literature, although not until later in the century.

Trying to Preserve the Past

In the meantime, America's writers were responding to other aspects of the changes sweeping the nation. As Americans began migrating to cities, many men and women of letters became disturbed that memories of an earlier way of life would be lost. Two literary movements, realism and regionalism, had grown during the last half of the nineteenth century and the beginning of the twentieth century in response to these changes.

Realism was an attempt to preserve an accurate record of the way life was in times past; regionalism was an attempt to preserve an image of America before industrialization drove people to the nation's cities to seek work in the new factories of the North. Even more dramatic changes were in store for America and the world, however, and these events produced and influenced the greatest American authors of the twentieth century.

In 1914 disagreements that had been building between European powers for decades erupted into the massive conflict now known as World War I. As Germany fought against England and France, the United States was increasingly pressured to become involved in the war. Finally, after repeated incidents in which Germany violated American neutrality, the United States entered the war on the side of England and France.

Immigrants flocked to America in the early twentieth century, many of them coming from diverse cultures.

The Growth of Modernism

American participation in World War I gave writers a chance to depict war in a realistic fashion that was shocking even to readers accustomed to the the horrors of war depicted by writers in earlier eras. As the editors of *The Norton Anthology of American Literature* note, the war "involved American artists and thinkers with the brutal actualities of large-scale modern war, so different from imaginary heroism."[3]

As a result of U.S. involvement in the war, Americans in general and many writers in particular began to feel a sense that they had lost their way. Literature professor Nancy Baym made the following observation regarding the effect of World War I on the way Americans viewed the world: "The senses of a great civilization being destroyed or destroying itself, of social breakdown, and of individual powerlessness became part of the American experience as a result of its participation in World War I, with resulting feelings of fear, disorientation, and on occasion, liberation."[4] Seeing vast portions of Europe destroyed and hundreds of thousands of people slaughtered left many Americans with the feeling that their lives were at the mercy of events and forces beyond their control.

Social critics of the day dubbed this feeling of being cut loose from familiar ideas "the Modern Temper," and it is this sense of social disorientation that readers see in the works of writers such as Ernest Hemingway. Literary critics consider the literature that was produced during these years to be part of the modernism movement. Ironically, many American writers of this era chose to live outside the United States. Hemingway, for example, lived in Europe for nearly two years, working on short stories and reporting for the *Toronto Star*.

World War I ended in 1918, and although life in the United States did not quite return to the ways of the previous decade, in some respects it was similar: Migrations of people from the country to the city continued, for example. Immigration to the United States also continued—this time by people displaced by the world war. Again, writers and artists responded to these changes by creating works that celebrated life as it existed in more isolated regions of the country that were untouched (or at least unchanged) by events elsewhere. William Faulkner, for instance, recreated the life of the late-nineteenth-century south; John Steinbeck's works depicted life in rural California, where the rhythms of life continued as they had in decades past.

A New Renaissance

The decade that followed World War I was a prosperous one. For some, however, that prosperity was never a reality. African Americans, suffering under the oppression of legalized segregation, did not as a group share in the general wealth of the times. Many blacks responded by leaving the rural South for the relative prosperity of northern cities, settling in large numbers in still-segregated neighborhoods such as Harlem in New York City.

Among these urban immigrants were some who would become widely read and respected poets, artists, and musicians. The explosion of artistic creativity among New York's African Americans is known today as the Harlem Renaissance. In the words of

A Salvation Army worker writes a letter to the family of a soldier wounded in World War I.

The Cotton Club, a jazz club during the Harlem Renaissance, provided musicians with an opportunity to showcase their talents.

one literature professor, "The so-called Harlem Renaissance involved the attempt of African American artists in many media to develop a strong cultural presence in America, both to demonstrate that black artists could equal white artists in their achievements and to articulate [speak about] their own cultural traditions and values."[5]

The prosperity of the 1920s was short-lived, however, and the year 1929 brought with it the worldwide economic collapse known as the Great Depression. The misery visited upon people across the nation was the greatest in living memory. Even families that had been well-to-do found themselves homeless; families that had been struggling to make ends meet before the Great Depression found that their previous pain had been only a taste of what was to come. The mood of despair that the hard times caused was reflected in much of the literature of the day. As one historian writes, "American fiction of the early depression era exuded disillusionment, cynicism, and despair, challenging the fundamental premises of American ideology."[6]

War and Disaffection

As the depression wore on, events elsewhere in the world intervened to distract at least some of America's attention from its desperate situation at home. By the mid-1930s it was increasingly clear that yet another massive war was coming. Spain was wracked by a civil war between Fascists trying to overthrow the government and Loyalists intent on retaining a fragile democracy. Germany again was making threats against its neighbors; and in the east, Japanese troops were marching into China. It seemed that the darkest views that writers depicted of human nature were justified. Some American writers and intellectuals rallied to the cause of those fighting against Fascism. Hemingway, for example, recalled, "The Spanish Civil War offered something which you could believe in wholly and completely, and in which you felt an absolute brotherhood with the others who were engaged in it."[7] The war in Spain, however, proved to be just a warm-up exercise for a conflagration that would change the world forever.

The war that came to be known as World War II led to permanent changes in American society. Women left traditional jobs as homemakers to aid the country's war effort by working in factories and other previously male-dominated careers. African Americans similarly found opportunity filling jobs that had previously been reserved for whites. With the end of the war, neither group was willing to see life return to the way it had been previously.

New Wealth—for Some

The end of World War II brought with it a time of unprecedented prosperity for the United States. World markets were now open to American goods, and with much of the rest of the world's industries in ruin, America had virtually no competition for the sale of manufactured goods. The late 1940s and early 1950s were seen by many as the best of times. It seemed that the economic "pie" was limitless—that there was enough for everyone. Many Americans saw the gaining of wealth to be the greatest goal that anyone could achieve. For many, a home in the suburbs, a stable (if not always stimulating) job, and a new car every other year represented the pinnacle of the American dream. And often, Americans viewed with suspicion anyone who believed otherwise. Some writers saw the American dream as an illusion, however. Arthur Miller, for example, wrote his play *Death of a Salesman* partly because he saw tragedy in the shallow pursuit of material wealth. His hero, Willy Loman, participates in that tragedy by pursuing—in vain—what many Americans would have termed *the good life*.

The appearance of limitless opportunity was, of course, an illusion. There were many who did not share in the bounty. In particular, African Americans often found that although jobs were available, the nature of those jobs was menial. Legalized segregation was still practiced throughout the United States and made any but the least desirable jobs off-limits to African Americans. And because educational opportunities were limited for African Americans, they often discovered that even when better jobs were open to them, the means to gain the necessary training for those jobs was unavailable.

American families prospered economically in the late 1940s and early 1950s.

In response to segregation, some African Americans resisted the restrictions on exercising their constitutional rights, ushering in what is known as the civil rights movement. In 1955, when a black seamstress named Rosa Parks refused to give up her seat to a white man on a bus in Montgomery, Alabama, more than a decade and a half of rapid—sometimes violent—change ensued. African Americans told their white fellow citizens in no uncertain terms that it was time to end segregation. Sit-ins, boycotts, and protest marches were used to drive home that message. Whites, particularly in the South, responded violently, and the late 1950s and the 1960s became a time when news reports frequently featured clashes between those who favored civil rights for everyone and those who felt that civil rights should be reserved for whites.

Searching for an American Literature

While some Americans were gradually becoming aware of how diverse their nation really was, many American writers of the

1950s were arguing that literature really could represent an entire nation. As one English professor writes, "Writers assumed that a short story, a novel, or a play could represent the experiences of an entire people, that a common national essence lay beneath distinctions of gender, race, ethnicity, religion, or region."[8] As the 1950s drew to a close, however, it became clear that America was far too diverse to adopt a single literary style.

Ironically, the prosperity of the 1950s and early 1960s contributed to the end of the sense of America as a uniform society. Americans who had been born in the years just after World War II,

Civil rights leader Martin Luther King Jr. (left) fought against segregation during the 1950s and 1960s.

known as the baby boom generation, found themselves with plenty of leisure time to pursue activities that interested them. Moreover, they had the money to pay for material goods they wanted. Unlike members of previous generations, who might have found their options for career and home life limited by economic circumstances, many Americans who were becoming adults in the late 1960s had the luxury of choosing other options. As one historian explains, "The fifties also bred cultural restiveness and a search for self-definition among adolescents. Few adults considered the implications of widespread affluence or the consequences of having a generation of teenagers who could stay in school instead of working."[9]

This break from traditional ideas about adult roles and careers certainly changed—and occasionally disrupted—society. It would also be reflected in the work of American writers. According to English professor Nina Baym, "As more became known about the world itself, the writer's ability to make sense of the whole was challenged."[10] The world was proving to be far more complex than many past writers had portrayed it.

Baym suggests that American literature reflects this complexity in its diversity of style: "A hallmark of the postwar period is its shift from unity as an ideal to diversity, and during these times American writing has been characterized by a great variety of styles all employed at the same time."[11] In Baym's view, however, even though late-twentieth-century writers began experimenting with many different writing styles, many of them share a common belief that language can be a literary tool every bit as powerful as such traditional elements as plot or characterization. Writers like Toni Morrison make special efforts to let language help them picture the world about which they write through the use of vivid imagery and metaphors.

Questioning Some Basic Assumptions

The increasing diversity of American culture that spawned a more diverse literature also led Americans, particularly members of some minority groups, to challenge some basic assumptions about American society. Some African Americans, for example, began asking why it was taking so long to achieve equal access to jobs and education; Native Americans and Mexican Americans asked similar questions and began demanding a fair share of the American dream.

Just as significantly, women, too, began to question assumptions about their role in American society. In 1963 a report by President John F. Kennedy's Presidential Commission on the Status of Women concluded that women also suffered from discrimination. In response to widespread bias against them in the workplace,

A man holds out a sign expressing his disapproval of NOW while pro-choice activists march down a street in Cincinnati.

women who served on the presidential commission formed the National Organization for Women (NOW). This new group lobbied members of Congress for laws to protect women's rights to equal employment opportunities; NOW also worked to bring public opinion to bear on women's rights and fought in the nation's courts against workplace discrimination.

The pressure applied by NOW and other organizations working on behalf of women eventually succeeded. By the end of the 1960s, as one historian writes, "The changed consciousness of the feminist movement opened a larger world of choices and opportunities for American women. Domesticity remained an option, but it was no longer the *only* option."[12]

As women were making political gains, the civil rights movement, which had been helping African Americans gain equality in job opportunities, education, and politics, helped give rise to the black arts movement, which brought many new African American writers to the attention of the reading public. As the political gains on the part of black Americans in the 1960s were consolidated, female African American authors gained particular attention; writers such as Toni Morrison and Alice Walker, for example, first achieved fame in the late 1970s and early 1980s.

Fragmenting of the American Dream

The resistance of African Americans to bigotry and discrimination helped fuel other political movements as well. As the 1960s wore on, students on college campuses across the country took a cue from the civil rights movement to protest what they saw as another massive injustice: the increasingly bloody war in the then little-known Asian nation of Vietnam. The United States had been involved in Vietnam since the early 1950s, first by giving monetary aid to the French, who had colonized the country and were fighting rebels who sought independence. Following the final withdrawal of the French from the country, the United States became directly involved, trying to prevent a takeover of the entire nation by Communists. Although Americans at first supported their government's efforts at stopping the spread of Communism, public opinion gradually turned against the war as more American soldiers died and little or no progress appeared to be made against the Communist troops.

The participants in these protests were overwhelmingly young. Dressed in ragged blue jeans or old military fatigues, many rejected the values their parents held. In the words of historian Theodore Roszak, these young adults were "a 'counter culture' . . . a culture so radically disaffiliated [divorced] from the mainstream assumptions of our society that it scarcely looks to many as a culture at all, but takes on the alarming appearance of a barbarian intrusion."[13]

In the closing decades of the twentieth century, writers began questioning even more basic assumptions about what constitutes truth. Authors began to promote the idea that literary works create realities of their own—realities that sometimes appear very different from the world the reader can observe, even though the settings may seem familiar. Writers such as Toni Morrison proved masterful at weaving these new realities through fiction that draws liberally on the supernatural.

New Realities, New Literatures

The future of American literature is uncertain as the twenty-first century dawns. It is likely that the literature of the United States will grow ever more diverse as the American people themselves increasingly celebrate the wide variety of traditions that make up American culture. New American writers come to the attention of their countrymen almost on a daily basis. But learning about those who came before is crucial to understanding the present.

CHAPTER 2

John Steinbeck: A Voice for the Dispossessed

Of all the American authors who were active in the twentieth century, John Steinbeck was perhaps most concerned about the poor and dispossessed. Steinbeck's career lasted forty years, and during those four decades he published some of the best-known and moving works in American literature. Most of Steinbeck's novels depict poor and downtrodden people of different races and ethnic groups struggling daily to overcome life's difficulties and tragedies. Although Steinbeck based his characters on men and women whom he had met and worked with, he was not himself from an underprivileged family.

An Early Passion for the Written Word

John Steinbeck III was born on February 27, 1902, in Salinas, California. John was the only son in a family of four children. John's father, John Ernst Steinbeck, was a mild-tempered man who worked as the manager of a flour mill in Salinas. His mother, Olive Hamilton Steinbeck, was a strong-willed woman who made most of the decisions in her family.

John's father was a shy man who was happy to live a life of quiet respectability. He was not, however, a particularly talented businessman, and when John was eight years old, the flour mill went bankrupt. The loss of John Ernst's job did not imperil the family financially, though. In fact, in material terms, the Steinbecks lived well. But the bankruptcy did affect the elder Steinbeck in other ways.

Early Influences

The career setbacks that John Ernst Steinbeck suffered did not help his home life—particularly his relationship with his children. Reluctant to take the lead in family matters, he gradually became ever more emotionally removed from his children. This distance was especially hard on young John. A neighbor of the Steinbecks, Mary Graydon, later recalled,

Mr. Steinbeck stayed in the background. He didn't play with John or the girls [John's sisters]. He seemed always in the shadows in the house, at the edge of things, lonely and depressed. Mrs. Steinbeck loved her son, but he was a little afraid of getting on the wrong side of her. He could never do anything right as far as she was concerned.[14]

Olive was close to her son, and her influence was significant. A schoolteacher by training, Olive was determined to make a reader of John. Not only did she read to him, but she also had him read to her from classic children's books. The Steinbecks subscribed to magazines such as the *Saturday Evening Post* and *National Geographic*, which John read in addition to such books as *Alice in Wonderland*.

A Difficult Adolescence

Steinbeck's childhood might seem ideal to some observers: a mother who cared about his education and a father who tried to provide financial security for his offspring. As he grew older, however, John began to suffer from the kinds of insecurity felt by many adolescents. These feelings were likely intensified by the fact that he was physically unattractive and slow to mature—his voice did not change until he was fifteen.

Despite feelings of insecurity, John participated in many high school activities. By the time he was a senior, he was elected president of the senior class and had served as associate editor of the school's yearbook. John's talent as a writer was recognized by his classmates, and he actually wrote a considerable portion of the yearbook himself. John's teachers also recognized his writing ability. One teacher, Ora M. Cupp, read his essays in class; another, Miss Hawkins, also praised and encouraged him.

Young Steinbeck was a talented student in English, and overall his grades were good. Upon his graduation in June 1919, John made plans to attend Stanford University the next fall. He chose Stanford because it was located close to home—no more than fifty miles away.

College Life

Steinbeck was unprepared for Stanford. He had not had to work particularly hard as a high school student, and the workload at Stanford was unexpectedly high. Moreover, Steinbeck was temperamentally unsuited to academic life, choosing to study only when it pleased him. He also chose to take only those courses that interested him, primarily courses in literature and writing. During his years at Stanford, Steinbeck adopted the habit of writing on a daily basis; he would maintain this practice for the rest of his life.

Although Steinbeck was not interested in many aspects of college life, he did enjoy writing and engaging in all-night conversations with his friends.

One aspect of college life that did appeal to Steinbeck was life in the college dormitory, where he enjoyed all-night conversations with other students and access to alcohol. In fact, according to biographer Jay Parini, it was in the dormitory "that [Steinbeck] began in earnest his long and troubled relationship with alcohol."[15] Alcohol would figure prominently in Steinbeck's life; for the next five decades, he would be a heavy drinker.

As the end of his first year at Stanford approached, Steinbeck looked forward to a summer job as a laborer at the Spreckle's Sugar Company. This summer's employment would eventually be valuable to Steinbeck since many of the characters that populate his novels are based on the people he worked with during this and subsequent stints with Spreckle's.

Poor Academic Performance

At the end of the summer, Steinbeck returned to Stanford, but he soon found that he was no better suited to academic life than he had been the previous year. His grades were abysmal, and by the end of the fall term he had been sent a letter announcing his dismissal from the university for poor academic performance. In the following years the young would-be writer drifted from job to job, meeting interesting people who would later become characters in future stories and novels.

Steinbeck would return to Stanford from time to time in the next few years, but he never was able to complete the requirements for an undergraduate degree. The pattern became familiar: He would spend a term or two at Stanford, followed by periods living with his parents in Salinas. Finally, in the spring of 1925, Steinbeck gave up on college once and for all.

Real Life

John Steinbeck's transition from college life to the outside world was eased when, through a friend, he got a job as a laborer at a resort on Lake Tahoe, located in the Sierra Nevada mountains. The work Steinbeck did varied depending on his boss's needs: Sometimes he would run errands; other times he would serve as chauffeur for the lodge's guests. In his free time, Steinbeck hammered away on his old typewriter, working on short stories. The resort would prove to be a periodic haven for Steinbeck, who would return there periodically to work.

Summer drew to an end, and with it the job at the resort. Somehow sensing that New York was the place for an aspiring writer to live, Steinbeck made his way there. Upon arriving in New York in December 1925, Steinbeck found life hard: His first job was as an unskilled laborer on a construction project. The heavy labor left him too exhausted at the end of each day to even read, much less write.

With help from an uncle, Joe Hamilton, Steinbeck got a job as a reporter for the *New York American*. Steinbeck later recalled, "I worked for the *American* and was assigned to the Federal Court in the old Park Row post office where I perfected my bridge game and did some lousy reporting. I did, however, perfect a certain literary versatility."[16] The job did not last long, though, as Steinbeck proved to lack the discipline necessary to find and write stories. He was soon fired since he spent far more time wandering around the streets of New York than he did following up on stories he had been assigned to cover.

First Hope

Through another friend, Steinbeck met Guy Holt, an editor at the small publishing house Robert M. McBride and Company. Holt liked the short stories Steinbeck showed him and told the young writer that if he could write six more of them, he would publish them as a collection. Steinbeck, naturally, was thrilled, and responded by quickly writing the requested stories. Unfortunately, by the time Steinbeck had finished his manuscript, he found that Guy Holt had left McBride for a much smaller firm, where short stories were of no interest. Holt urged Steinbeck to get to work on a novel instead. Steinbeck left Holt's office vowing that he would return some day, with a novel in hand.

His stay in New York a failure, Steinbeck returned to California. After brief reunions with his parents and friends in the Palo Alto area, Steinbeck headed once more for Lake Tahoe. Again with the help of

Trees grow near Lake Tahoe, the resort city where Steinbeck briefly worked.

friends, he landed a job as the caretaker on a large estate on the southern shore of Lake Tahoe owned by Alice Brigham. The winter, when Mrs. Brigham and her family were away, offered Steinbeck what he most needed: solitude. Alone, he worked on a novel about the English buccaneer Henry Morgan titled *Cup of Gold*. This work would prove to be his first success.

Steinbeck stayed in the Lake Tahoe area for the better part of two years, working first for the Brigham family and then for a fish hatchery. It was at the fish hatchery that Steinbeck met the young woman who would become his first wife. Carol Henning arrived at the hatchery one day for a tour. Steinbeck was immediately taken with the pretty young woman, and she returned his attentions. The two spent as much time as they could together until Henning returned to her home in San Francisco. Steinbeck intended to see more of her, and she encouraged that idea.

The fall of 1928 found Steinbeck in San Francisco. He got a job, again as a laborer, in a warehouse in the city. The warehouse job, as might be expected, was exhausting. With little time or energy available, Steinbeck had completed work on *Cup of Gold* and was at work on his next novel, tentatively titled *The Green Lady*, but the process went slowly. Money was tight, but Steinbeck's father came to his rescue, offering him the use of the family's cottage in Pacific Grove. In addition, John Ernst Steinbeck gave his son at least twenty-five dollars a month in spending money. With this help, the young author was able to keep working on his novel.

Living in the cottage in Pacific Grove proved a benefit in another way as well. The privacy allowed Steinbeck the opportunity to spend time with Carol Henning when she visited on the weekends. The young couple spent their time together playing tennis and hunting crabs along the rocky shoreline near Monterey.

Success at Last

It was while Steinbeck was living in Pacific Grove that he heard the kind of news that every would-be writer dreams of: Robert M. McBride and Company had agreed to accept his novel *Cup of Gold*. Steinbeck correctly expected that his first book would not earn him much money. For this reason, he continued to discourage the idea of marriage, even though Henning was growing more insistent.

Late in the fall of 1929, however, Steinbeck and Henning announced their intention to get married, although they declined to set a wedding date. Henning proved to be an excellent companion for Steinbeck: She willingly spent a great deal of time typing his manuscripts and making suggestions for improvements. More importantly, Henning, despite the wealth and privilege she had grown up with, cared deeply about the poor and disadvantaged people in America. This social awareness helped Steinbeck develop his own social conscience.

Marriage

As 1929 drew to a close, Steinbeck moved closer to making good his intention to marry Henning. In December of that year, the young couple headed south, bound for Los Angeles, where they planned to be married in a civil ceremony. The journey took longer than expected, though, due to frequent stops to repair the old car they were driving. Finally, in January 1930 the couple arrived in Los Angeles, where they moved in temporarily with Steinbeck's old friend Dook Sheffield and his wife, Maryon. On January 14, 1930, John Steinbeck and Carol Henning were married in a civil ceremony in Glendale, California. The Sheffields were the only witnesses to the event.

The Steinbecks set up housekeeping in a tiny house in the town of Eagle Rock, located near Los Angeles. This was not a good time for a struggling writer. All of America had spiraled into the hard times of the Great Depression. Carol tried to get secretarial jobs in Los Angeles, but without success. As the summer of 1930 drew to a close, the Steinbecks packed their belongings into their car and headed back to the only place they could afford: Pacific Grove and the cottage the Steinbeck family owned there. Of this time, Steinbeck later recalled, "The Depression was no financial shock to me. I didn't have any money to lose, but in common with millions I did dislike hunger and cold."[17] Fortunately, there was plenty to eat in the form of seafood that could be caught and vegetables that could be grown year-round. Steinbeck managed to keep himself and Carol warm by building fires from the driftwood he collected on the nearby beach each day.

Steinbeck's marriage began to deteriorate when his wife became attracted to his friend Joseph Campbell (pictured).

New Hope, New Strains

While he and Carol were living in Pacific Grove, Steinbeck had been working steadily on a collection of short stories titled *The Pastures of Heaven*. By sheer chance, it was on Steinbeck's birthday, February 27, 1932, that he learned that the firm of Cape and Smith had agreed to publish the collection. Better still, the editor, Robert O. Ballou, offered Steinbeck a contract to publish his next two books as well. This was the beginning of a long relationship between the two men.

Just as Steinbeck's career was going in the right direction, it seemed that his marriage was headed the opposite way. Steinbeck became aware that Carol had become attracted to one of his friends, Joseph Campbell (who would go on to become famous for his research on mythology). Steinbeck's jealousy over the relationship damaged the Steinbecks' marriage.

Despite his marital difficulties, the 1930s proved to be a productive time for Steinbeck. During these years he completed work on some of the novels and short story collections for which he is best known. *Tortilla Flat*, a brief novel about Mexican Americans living in Monterey, was completed in 1934; *In Dubious Battle*, about efforts of migrant workers to fight exploitation by landowners, was essentially finished by early 1935; and by early 1937 *Of Mice and Men*, a novel about two hoboes who dream of owning their own ranch, was ready for publication. Even more important, however, was the assignment Steinbeck received in 1936 to write a series of articles for the *San Francisco News* about the plight of migrant farmworkers in California. These workers, who had once been the owners of small farms in places like Oklahoma, were now in desperate straits after having been forced off of family farms by a combination of terrible drought and poor economic conditions. In one of his articles, Steinbeck writes,

> Thousands of them are crossing the borders in ancient rattling automobiles, destitute and hungry and homeless, ready to accept any pay so that they may eat and feed their children. . . .
>
> They arrive in California usually having used up every resource to get here, even to the selling of the poor blankets

In 1936 Steinbeck received an assignment to write a series of articles about the plight of migrant farmworkers.

and utensils and tools on the way to buy gasoline. They arrive bewildered and beaten and usually in a state of semi-starvation, with only one necessity to face immediately, and that is to find work at any wage in order that the family may eat.[18]

Fame

While Steinbeck was working on his assignment for the *San Francisco News*, *Of Mice and Men* was becoming a best-seller. The popularity of this short work did much to enhance Steinbeck's reputation. Unfortunately, Steinbeck was shy and uncomfortable with all of the publicity that the book generated for him. And far greater fame awaited.

As the 1930s closed, Steinbeck's success seemed assured. *Of Mice and Men* had been made into a successful stage play, and by May 1938 he was hard at work on what he was sure would be his most important novel, *The Grapes of Wrath*. The novel dealt movingly with the hardships endured by the people Steinbeck had observed while on assignment for the *San Francisco News*. Considering the impact the book was to have, the speed with which Steinbeck wrote the novel is astonishing: By October 26, 1938, he had completed it. Steinbeck's life thereafter would never be the same.

The Grapes of Wrath was published in the spring of 1939 and received generally positive reviews. Steinbeck had been cautious in his expectations, warning his editor, Pat Covici, not to have too many copies printed. Such caution was unwarranted: By the end of the year *The Grapes of Wrath* had sold well over four hundred thousand copies. In the more than sixty years since its publication, the novel has become a staple in libraries and classrooms around the world.

More Hard Times

The Grapes of Wrath assured Steinbeck's place in American literature. Indeed, in 1940 he was awarded one of the most prestigious honors of all, the Pulitzer Prize for fiction. In his private life, however, the situation was less happy. His marriage to Carol was essentially finished. Steinbeck had been living with another woman, Gwen Conger, for some time, and they had been planning to marry once his marriage to Carol had been officially dissolved. Finally, in the spring of 1943, John and Carol Steinbeck's divorce became final. Despite being free to marry Gwen, Steinbeck was not happy, observing, "I can't say there was any joy in that final decree. In fact, it snapped me back into all the bad times of the last years. The final failure of an association."[19]

Once the divorce from Carol became final, Steinbeck and Conger married almost immediately, on March 29, 1943. Their time together as newlyweds was cut short, however, as Steinbeck received permission to travel overseas to report on the Allies' efforts in World War II. By the end of June, he was in London. Gwen was left behind; it was not a good start for a marriage.

The intrusion of World War II into the Steinbecks' marriage proved one of many times that Gwen had to accept that her husband's work came ahead of his relationship with her. Over the course of five years, the Steinbecks' marriage deteriorated, and by the end of the summer of 1948, the couple had signed a separation agreement. Steinbeck and Gwen had produced two children: Thom, born in August 1944, and John IV, born in June 1946.

In spite of his troubled personal life, the years since the publication of *The Grapes of Wrath* had been good ones professionally for Steinbeck. He had been completing an average of one book per year, including some that would become famous in their own right, such as *Cannery Row*, a brief novel about the people who inhabited the waterfront in Monterey, and *The Pearl*, a novella about a poor Mexican fisherman who finds a pearl of immense value. Moreover, further honors were coming his way. In late 1948 he was elected to the American Academy of Arts and Letters, an exclusive group of writers and artists whose purpose is to promote the development of art and literature in America. To be selected to join this group was flattering since its members included such highly respected literary figures as Mark Twain, Edith Wharton, and William Faulkner.

A New Beginning

As the 1950s opened, Steinbeck's personal fortunes had again improved. His relationship with Elaine Scott, the former wife of Zachary Scott, a well-known actor, developed, and on December 28, 1950, they were married. Although Gwen did not care for Elaine, she did allow her sons, Thom and John, to visit their father and his new wife regularly.

In addition to a new marriage, Steinbeck was working hard on a new novel. Tentatively titled *The Salinas Valley*, it was a blend of fiction and autobiography. Steinbeck wrote in a letter, "I am choosing to write this book to my sons. They are little boys now and they will

Gwen Conger sang on the radio before her marriage to Steinbeck.

never know what they came from through me, unless I tell them. . . . I want them to know how it was, I want to tell them directly, and perhaps by speaking directly to them I shall speak directly to other people."[20] The writing proceeded steadily, and by the end of February 1952 he had completed work on the novel, by then titled *East of Eden*. The novel was published early in the fall of 1952 and almost immediately rose to the top of the bestseller lists. (In a testimonial to the power that Steinbeck's name had by this time, the prepublication orders for the book had exceeded one hundred thousand copies.)

Warning Signs

Following the publication of *East of Eden*, Steinbeck and his wife decided in the spring of 1954 to take an extended trip to Europe, mostly to give Steinbeck a chance to rest from the intense effort that writing the novel had required. One of the last items of business before departing was to have a physical examination, which was necessary because Steinbeck wanted to purchase life insurance for himself. The results of the physical were unsettling: The doctor told him that his heart was unusually small for a man of his size, which meant that it was being strained.

The news about his heart depressed Steinbeck, but even more worrisome was the spell he suffered not long after while he and Elaine were traveling in France. En route to Paris, Steinbeck suddenly felt weak and then lapsed into unconsciousness. Although a doctor who examined him diagnosed this episode as sunstroke, it is now thought that this was probably a minor stroke. This incident upset both Steinbeck and his wife, although Steinbeck's spirits improved somewhat after a cardiologist in Paris examined him and reassured him about the condition of his heart.

The Steinbecks left Europe in December 1954 aboard an ocean liner bound for New York and arrived home just before Christmas. The Steinbecks needed a place to live, so in February 1955 they bought a home near the town of Sag Harbor on Long Island. Although the house needed renovation, it suited Steinbeck well. Elaine later recalled, "What John liked was the fact that the house had possibilities. It had yet to be imagined. The main thing about it was really the sea. John had been longing to live near the water."[21]

The Winter of Our Discontent

Steinbeck continued to work on a number of projects throughout the late 1950s, but he appeared to be having difficulty finding the one book that would capture his imagination and that of critics and readers. More ominously, Steinbeck's health was becoming more precarious.

Late in 1959 Steinbeck had a close call when, while smoking in bed, he suffered another ministroke and passed out. His wife, smelling smoke, found him unconscious amid smoldering bed linens. Fortunately, Steinbeck was not seriously injured, and he was soon back to work on his next project, a novel titled *The Winter of Our Discontent*.

The theme of Steinbeck's new novel was what he considered the increasing and destructive obsession among Americans with material wealth. In June 1961 *The Winter of Our Discontent* was published and received generally positive reviews. One critic, Carlos Baker, wrote in the *New York Times Book Review*, that it was "a highly readable novel which bristles with disturbing ideas as a spring garden bristles with growing shoots."[22]

The Nobel Prize

The Winter of Our Discontent turned out to be Steinbeck's last novel. Increasingly, he was troubled by fatigue, and he continued to experience minor strokes. The summer of 1962 saw the publication of *Travels with Charley*, which was a nonfiction account of a trip he took around America accompanied by his dog, Charley. Almost immediately, the book rose to the top of the best-seller list. The public response to Steinbeck's work was to be dwarfed, however, by the honor that awaited him that fall.

The fall of 1962 was a tense one for the entire world since the United States and the Soviet Union were in the midst of a major dispute over the USSR's decision to place nuclear missiles in Cuba. Like many around the world, Steinbeck was watching televised reports on the crisis when an unrelated news item was announced: John Steinbeck had been awarded the Nobel Prize for literature.

Travels with Charley—*Steinbeck's nonfiction account of the trip he took around America with his dog, Charley (pictured)—was published in 1962.*

The Nobel Prize for literature is awarded annually and is considered the highest honor a writer can receive. In Steinbeck's case, however, the honor was diminished somewhat by the reaction of many critics, who felt that the prize should have gone to someone who had more recently produced what they deemed a major literary work. Steinbeck tried to shrug off such criticism, but he was naturally hurt to read that critics believed that his best years as a novelist were behind him.

The Steinbecks headed for Stockholm, Sweden, to receive the Nobel Prize in December 1962. Part of the award ceremony was the acceptance speech, which Steinbeck used to voice his belief in humankind as the best hope for planet Earth: "Man himself has become our greatest hazard and our only hope. So that today, Saint John the Apostle may well be paraphrased: In the end is the *word*, and the word is *man*, and the word is *with* man."[23]

John Steinbeck poses with his 1962 Nobel Prize in Stockholm, Sweden.

A Quiet End

As the 1960s wore on Steinbeck stayed active, although no more novels were forthcoming. He spent three months in 1967 traveling in South Vietnam as a correspondent for *Newsday*, reporting on the war that American forces were fighting there. By the fall of that year, however, he was in agonizing pain from deteriorating disks in his back. As 1968 dawned, other longtime health problems reappeared: He suffered repeated ministrokes, in July he suffered a mild heart attack, and in November he began experiencing difficulty breathing due to emphysema. On December 20 Elaine Steinbeck spent the day with her husband, reading to him and reminiscing with him about past happy times together. Late in the afternoon, Elaine lay on the bed beside Steinbeck; just before five-thirty, he gradually dropped into a coma and stopped breathing.

John Steinbeck's ashes were buried in his family's cemetery plot in Salinas, California. His memory lives on in libraries and on bookshelves all around the world. Although some critics continue to question the quality of his work, the challenges that Steinbeck poses for his readers enliven debates about enduring social problems and humanity's answers to them.

CHAPTER 3

Ernest Hemingway: The Solitary Hero

Perhaps no American author embodied more qualities that fall under the heading of "red-blooded American male" than Ernest Hemingway did. Tall and robust, Hemingway was an outdoorsman, an athlete, and a consummate storyteller. Whether he was hunting in Africa, carousing in the bars of Paris or Havana, or reporting on wars in Spain or China, Ernest Hemingway exuded a vigor and drive that most people can only wish for. More than most men and women of letters, Hemingway's life was filled with genuine adventure; the beginnings of that life, however, were fairly ordinary.

Ernest Miller Hemingway was born on July 21, 1899, the second child of Clarence "Ed" and Grace Hemingway. The elder Hemingways named their son after his maternal grandfather, Ernest Hall, and his great uncle, Miller Hall. Over the coming years, another four siblings would be born; the one disappointment for young Ernest was that he would have to wait some years before he would be joined at last by a brother.

The Hemingway family was well-off by the standards of the day. Clarence Hemingway made a comfortable living as a general practitioner, which brought the family a reliable (if modest) income. Grace Hemingway eventually inherited her parents' house, which she was able to sell; the money from the sale of this inheritance went to build and furnish a large and comfortable home in the town of Oak Park, Illinois.

Despite their comparative wealth, the elder Hemingways argued frequently over money—and over how their children should be raised. While Clarence tended to be strict, Grace saw discipline as having the potential of stifling creativity. As Ernest grew older, he learned from his father that rules were to be obeyed; from his mother, he learned that life was to be enjoyed and that part of that enjoyment was attending symphonic concerts, operas, and art exhibitions in nearby Chicago.

Young Ernest was introduced to books early. One of his favorites was a collected volume of a monthly magazine titled *Birds of Nature*. Perhaps in a prediction of things to come, Ernest also loved to listen as stories were told to him. He took a particular liking to stories about owls after he saw one perched in a tree near his house.

In addition to being interested in nature, little Ernest showed a tenderness towards living things. As his mother once noted, Ernest cried "bitterly over the death of a fly he had tried to revive on sugar and water."[24]

Ernest also learned from his father the love of the natural world that would later be so much a part of his stories and novels. As biographer Carlos Baker notes,

> The boy's later memories of his father were nearly always in outdoor settings—flushing jacksnipe on the prairies; walking through dead grass or harvest fields where corn stood in shocks; passing by grist or cider mills or trickling lumber dams. He thought of his father whenever he saw a lake or an open fire or a horse and buggy or a flight of wild geese, or whenever there was wood to be split or water to be hauled.[25]

High School

Ernest's boyhood passed in an idyllic manner: He was loved and protected by his parents, he pleased his teachers, and he spent his summers at the family's cottage in northern Michigan. As the time neared for Ernest to enter high school, he worried greatly that he was still small for his age. It was not until the summer after his freshman year that he began to get his adolescent growth, but he made up for lost time that summer and grew several inches in just three or four months. He would, by his graduation three years later, stand nearly six feet tall.

Ernest first began to show promise as a writer in high school. As a sophomore, he wrote a couple of short stories that were good enough to be published in his high school's literary magazine, the *Tabula*. He also began working as a reporter for the school's newspaper, the *Trapeze*. The experience as a high school journalist would shortly lead him to his first real job.

Off to Kansas City

After graduating from high school in June 1917, young Hemingway had several options: He could go to college, he could go into the army and fight in the world war then raging in Europe, or he

From an early age, Ernest Hemingway had a strong appreciation of nature and enjoyed being outdoors.

could go to work. Hemingway chose the last of these options, and through the influence of an uncle in Kansas City, he landed a job as a reporter for the *Kansas City Star*. His beat consisted of Kansas City's 15th Street police station, Union Station, and the General Hospital.

Hemingway liked his work for the *Star*, but it was largely routine and he longed for action. The war in Europe offered the possibility of real adventure, but there were at least a couple of obstacles: His father was opposed to his enlisting in the Army, and his poor eyesight made it unlikely that he would be accepted. A friendship with another young reporter, Theodore Brumback, helped him find the route to war that he so wanted. Brumback had spent the summer of 1917 as an ambulance driver in France; he told Hemingway stories that made life in Europe seem romantic.

Brumback, Hemingway, and a third friend at the *Star*, Wilson Hicks, applied to the Red Cross as ambulance drivers.

Off to the Great War

In late May 1918 Hemingway arrived in France and was soon shipped to Italy, where he was assigned to Section Four of the American Red Cross. For three weeks Hemingway drove an ambulance, ferrying wounded soldiers from the front to aid stations away from the fighting. Hemingway found the work boring; he longed for more direct involvement in the war. He soon got his wish.

During World War I, Hemingway worked as an ambulance driver for the Red Cross.

While visiting the trenches where an Italian infantry unit was hunkered down, Hemingway was seriously wounded when an Austrian artillery shell exploded near his position. Hit in the legs by shrapnel, Hemingway was barely able to walk. However, he still managed to rescue an Italian soldier who was even more badly wounded. The situation grew worse when, as he was carrying his charge toward safety, Hemingway was hit in the right leg by fire from a machine gun. Just short of his nineteenth birthday, Hemingway found himself in the Red Cross hospital in Milan, Italy, awaiting surgery to remove two machine gun slugs and a great deal of shrapnel from his legs.

Hemingway's recovery from his wounds was slow, but his time in the hospital was made less unpleasant by the presence of one nurse in particular, Agnes von Kurowsky. The young man fell in love with this pretty, tall woman with dark hair. During the time he remained in Italy, Hemingway saw as much of von Kurowsky as he could. Von Kurowsky, however, encouraged him to return to his home in the United States, perhaps sensing that nothing permanent could come of their relationship.

Back Home

Ernest Hemingway did as Agnes von Kurowsky asked and returned to his home in Oak Park in January 1919. In his parents' home, Hemingway slowly recovered from his war wounds. He spent time with old friends and went on several camping trips in northern Michigan that summer, one of which would become the basis for one of his best-known short stories, "Big Two-Hearted River."

For the next year Hemingway showed little sign of settling down. He spent several months in early 1920 working as a feature writer for the *Toronto Star*, and he spent much of the summer carousing with his friends in northern Michigan. Then, in October, he met Elizabeth "Hadley" Richardson. That meeting soon developed into friendship, which in turn led to courtship; they were wed on September 3, 1921.

Life in Europe

The Hemingways set out to make a life for themselves in Chicago. Although Hemingway had been working at his writing, he was earning little money, and the young couple was living on income from Hadley's inheritance from her mother. It seemed, therefore, like a perfect solution when Hemingway's friend, the already-famous author Sherwood Anderson, suggested that they move to Paris. Life there was inexpensive, and an aspiring writer could benefit from being in a city alive with famous men and women of letters.

In December 1921 Ernest and Hadley Hemingway boarded an ocean liner bound for Paris. They settled down in a small apartment, and Hemingway began once again to write. He tried above all else for simplicity in his prose, saying, "All you have to do is write one true sentence. Write the truest sentence that you know."[26] Hemingway also began

Agnes von Kurowsky, the nurse whom Hemingway loved.

work as a correspondent for his former employer, the *Toronto Star*. For the next year and a half, he traveled around Europe reporting on events in Germany, Italy, and Spain.

Spain, in particular, captured Hemingway's imagination. Here, he saw his first bullfight. The bravery of the matadors, locked in a duel that could end in death for either bull or bullfighter, must have appealed to Hemingway's sense of heroism: A single person facing death. Bullfighting would be a recurring theme in some of Hemingway's best-known works in years to come.

A Productive Time

The next few years proved to be satisfying and productive ones for Hemingway. He completed work on a short story that would one day become his most famous, "Big Two-Hearted River"; a collection of short stories, *In Our Time*, was accepted for publication in 1925; and in September of that year he completed work on his first novel, *The Sun Also Rises*. Hemingway's second novel, *A Farewell to Arms*, was published in 1929.

One less-positive aspect of the 1920s was the strain Hemingway and Hadley experienced in their marriage. Hemingway, who had grown more distant from Hadley, had had an extramarital affair with Pauline Pfeiffer, an editor at *Vogue* magazine. Hadley eventually agreed to a divorce; Hemingway, in response, experienced tremendous guilt, telling one friend that he and Hadley were divorcing "because I'm a son of a bitch."[27] The marriage officially ended in January 1927; Hemingway, who was now free to follow his heart, married Pfeiffer in May of that same year.

A view of Hemingway's Spanish Colonial home in Key West, Florida. The Florida Keys fascinated Hemingway and influenced his writing.

A Man of Letters

As the 1930s opened, it seemed that Hemingway, even though he was only a little over thirty years of age, was established as "a man of letters." In the words of author Anthony Burgess, "Hemingway had arrived; he saw himself as one of the patriarchs of American literature, young as he was."[28] Hemingway felt this way despite the decidedly lukewarm reviews of his latest novel, *Death in the Afternoon*.

The 1930s also brought momentous changes to Hemingway's life. Pauline's uncle presented his niece and her husband with a house on Key West. This was a real boon to Hemingway. He spent his time there producing a number of novels, and his works based on life in the Florida Keys and in nearby Cuba would lead him to be revered as one of the greatest literary figures of the twentieth century.

Even more than Key West, Cuba proved to be a place where Hemingway found inspiration for his writing. It was during a lengthy vacation in Cuba in the winter of 1932 that a fishing guide told Hemingway the story of a fisherman who had battled to land a huge marlin but had lost the great fish to sharks. Always on the lookout for material that could be turned into a story, Hemingway filed the tale in his memory.

Not long after this trip, Hemingway decided to follow through on long-delayed plans to go on an African safari. As with his other foreign travels, this safari provided material for some of his best-known works.

For Whom the Bell Tolls

His trip to Africa could not long distract him from upsetting news from Spain. Hemingway had been in love with Spain since his first stay there in the early 1920s, and he was distressed to learn that the nation was in political chaos and seemed headed for civil war. Although he focused his attention on other concerns for a time, the situation in Spain would return to haunt Hemingway.

By 1937 the democratically elected Spanish government was under armed attack by Fascist rebels. Although other governments around the world remained officially neutral in the conflict, volunteers from a large number of nations had formed the International Brigade to help the Spanish government put down the rebellion. Hemingway headed for Spain to report on the war. What he saw of the war became the basis of his novel *For Whom the Bell Tolls*.

By the end of 1938, convinced that the Fascist rebels would win the civil war in Spain, Hemingway left the country. This was a difficult period for him. Not only had he seen Fascism overcome democracy, but his writing was not going well: A play he had written was being revised by its producers, and Hemingway was not satisfied with the changes. To top matters off, his marriage to Pauline was in deep trouble, largely because Hemingway had fallen in love with another woman, Martha Gellhorn.

Cuba

Although Hemingway's marriage was falling apart, he continued to work. Compared to the problems with his play *The Fifth Brigade*, work on his latest novel, *For Whom the Bell Tolls*, was going well. Hemingway took refuge from the confusion in his personal life by retreating to Cuba. There, he was joined by Gellhorn, who encouraged him to rent an estate about fifteen miles outside of Havana called Finca Vigia ("View Farm"). Eventually, he and Gellhorn would buy Finca Vigia; this would be Hemingway's haven for much of the rest of his life.

Settled in Cuba, Hemingway worked at attaining closure on a number of issues, both professional and personal. He completed *For Whom the Bell Tolls* in July 1940, and by that fall, when the novel was actually published, it was already a bestseller. With that project completed, Hemingway turned his attention to personal matters. Within weeks of finalizing his divorce from Pauline, Hemingway and Martha Gellhorn were married by a justice of the peace in Cheyenne, Wyoming.

Martha Gellhorn (pictured), who desired to pursue her career as a war correspondent, proved to be too independent for Hemingway's tastes.

A Short, Unhappy Marriage

The marriage to Martha was destined to be short. Hemingway's expectations of a submissive wife who would accommodate his erratic schedule was incompatible with Martha's independent nature and her desire to pursue her career as a war correspondent. The marriage lasted less than six years.

In March 1946 Hemingway was married for the fourth and final time to Mary Welsh, a writer whom he had met in Europe the previous year while writing about the final days of World War II.

Mary was surprisingly patient with her temperamental husband. Despite his tendency to get drunk frequently and openly pursue other, younger women, she stayed with him. When he became depressed over temporary bouts with writer's block, she stood by him. With Mary's support, Hemingway strove to complete what he saw as a lengthy trilogy: *The Sea When Young, The Sea When Absent*, and *The Sea in Being*.

The Old Man and the Sea

Hemingway never completed the trilogy, which was actually a very long, single novel in three parts. He did, however, decide to develop the story he had heard years ago about the fisherman who had lost his prize marlin to sharks. Writer Anthony

Mary Welsh, remained dedicated to Hemingway despite his alcoholism and depression.

Burgess evaluates this short novel, published as *The Old Man and the Sea*, as "a book that . . . restored his international reputation to the extent of his being considered worthy for the [Nobel Prize], that sold immensely, that moved ordinary people to tears, that is unquestionably a small masterpiece."[29]

The Old Man and the Sea was published in late 1952. The novella was an instant commercial success; Hemingway's fellow writers praised it as well. One Hemingway biographer, Richard B. Lyttle, reports, "William Faulkner said *The Old Man and the Sea* might prove to be the best book from the current generation of writers."[30] In the spring of 1953, Hemingway learned from news reports that his little novel had been awarded a very high honor, the Pulitzer Prize for fiction. This was, however, small in comparison to the honor that awaited him.

The Biggest Prize of All

The Hemingways celebrated the success of *The Old Man and the Sea* by going on a lengthy African safari. It was an adventure-filled trip, punctuated by encounters with a wounded rhinoceros, a dangerous brushfire, and a plane crash that nearly cost the couple their lives (and led to a number of premature reports of their deaths). After they returned to Cuba in the spring of 1954, Hemingway recuperated from his injuries suffered on the safari and began work on a series of short stories based on these recent experiences. During this period of recuperation, word came that Hemingway had been awarded the greatest prize of all: the Nobel Prize for literature.

Hemingway was both pleased and concerned by the news of this honor. Anthony Burgess reports that Hemingway held an intense dislike for the persons and work of two previous Nobel laureates, Sinclair Lewis and William Faulkner. "Moreover, 'no son of a bitch that ever won the Nobel Prize ever wrote anything worth reading afterwards,' he said before he got it."[31] Although events eventually proved him wrong, Hemingway was right in one respect: It would not be until after he was dead that another of his books would be published.

The Final Days

As the 1950s drew to a close, Hemingway's health was precarious and his writing was again going badly. He was overeating and drinking far too much. He blamed his inability to write on the fact that Mary had been injured in a fall and he had been obliged to do the housework. Hemingway worked fitfully on a book titled *The Dangerous Summer*, which *Life* magazine had agreed to publish in serial form.

Hemingway was also showing signs of mental problems. In particular, he displayed suspicion of people around him and became convinced that he had no money, which was not the case. A stay in a hospital where he could be treated for both psychological and physical disorders seemed in order, and Mary Hemingway authorized her husband's admission to the Mayo Clinic in Rochester, Minnesota. In addition to physical problems associated with heavy drinking, Hemingway was diagnosed with depression. He then began a course of treatment that included electroshock therapy.

The electroshock therapy appeared to have some benefit: Hemingway began to take an interest in those around him. He made friends with the doctors and nurses who were treating him, but he continued to show signs of paranoia. He imagined that someone was trying to take his money despite his belief that he had no money for anyone to take. Although he was still having some prob-

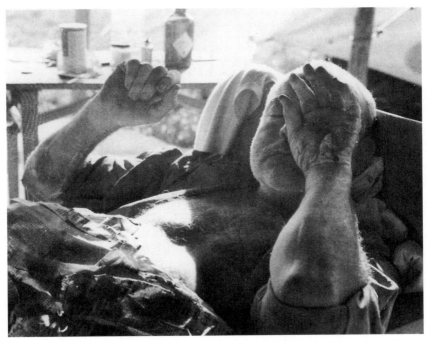

Toward the end of his life, Hemingway struggled with physical problems associated with his heavy drinking and depression.

lems, Hemingway was well enough to be discharged, and on January 22, 1961, he left the clinic for his home in Ketchum, Idaho.

The months immediately following his release were a bleak time for Hemingway and those around him. In addition to suffering from writer's block, he lost weight and worried that it was due to cancer. And to further complicate matters, one morning Mary Hemingway found her husband standing in his bathrobe, cradling a shotgun in his arms. She knew that he needed to be hospitalized again. Hemingway submitted to another course of electroshock therapy; convinced that he was improved, his doctors released him in late June and he returned home to Ketchum.

Only a few weeks later, on July 2, 1961, Ernest Hemingway awoke early one morning, put on his bathrobe, and walked downstairs. Unlocking the cabinet where his guns were kept, he chose a double-barrelled shotgun and loaded it. He then braced the stock against the floor, put the muzzle to his forehead, and pulled the triggers.

Hemingway's legacy is still being debated. Although some people criticize his work as glorifying negative qualities like insensitivity and violence, the directness of his writing and its celebration of heroic behavior continue to make him a favorite among readers of American literature.

CHAPTER 4

William Faulkner: A Son of the South

Most American authors built their reputations by speaking to the hopes, fears, and ideals of one or another segment of American society. Perhaps no one did this better than William Faulkner. A native of Mississippi, Faulkner used fiction filled with odd characters possessing wildly diverse voices and perspectives to portray the society of the Deep South. Through the inhabitants of the fictional Yoknapatawpha County, Faulkner gave voice to the poor and dispossessed of the South in the early twentieth century, as well as to those who recalled the decadent glory that had been the South prior to the Civil War. Faulkner constructed this world from what he saw and experienced daily; his characters' lives in many ways mirror Faulkner's own life.

A Troubled Family

William Faulkner was born on September 25, 1897, in the tiny town of New Albany, Mississippi, which boasted a population of 497. The Falkners (William added a "u" to the family name some years later) belonged to the social class known as the gentry, meaning that they were wealthy enough to employ servants. Since he did not need to work particularly hard to earn a living, William's father, Murry, was able to spend time with his son.

Murry Falkner loved two things above all else: the railroad that he worked for, which belonged to his father; and whiskey, which he consumed in considerable quantities each day. Murry alternated between being an angry, abusive drunk, and a gentle father who took his son on hunting trips and told him stories.

Young William's mother, Maud Falkner, was a stern woman who disapproved of her husband's drinking. Despite her distaste for what she saw as her husband's weakness, she stayed with him. Moreover, however unhappy she might have been, Maud Falkner refused to share her unhappiness with those around her—at least verbally. As biographer Stephen B. Oates notes, "She set an example of stoic resolve, summed up by the sign on the cupboard above her stove: 'DON'T COMPLAIN—DON'T EXPLAIN.'"[32]   Maud taught her son to read and instilled in him a love of literature.

Pulled in Different Directions

In addition to his parents, a number of adults were influential in William's early life, and for many years he suffered from a sense of being pulled in different directions by these people. A black servant, Caroline Barr—or Mammy Callie as she was known to William—looked after his day-to-day needs and told him stories about the Old South, slavery, the Civil War, and Reconstruction. And his grandfather, "the Young Colonel," as he was called, told William stories as well, particularly about his great-grandfather's exploits in the Civil War.

Early on, William showed signs of being quite a storyteller himself. One of his cousins later said of him, "It got so that when Billy [as he was known at the time] told you something, you never knew if it was the truth or just something he'd made up."[33] William also showed signs of becoming a poet, or perhaps an artist, and by the time he was a teenager he had submitted at least one drawing to a magazine for possible publication. His interest in poetry, along with a lack of interest in working at his chores, did not set well with other boys, who thought him odd. His bookishness and idleness also alienated his father, who thought he took after his mother.

Southern tenant farmers gather for a union meeting. Faulkner wrote about people and events he saw and experienced in the South.

Perhaps the most lasting influence on young William was that of family friend Phil Stone. This young man, although less than five years older than seventeen-year-old William, had studied literature at Yale and thought he saw real promise in William's poetry. He volunteered to tutor the younger man in literature. Under Stone's influence, William learned about the great English poets; the political life of post-Reconstruction Mississippi, and the people who would one day fill his novels. Among other topics, "Stone lectured . . . about postwar Mississippi politics and the rise of the rednecks—that new breed of acquisitive, unscrupulous farmers who had appeared after the Civil War."[34] William was completely taken with Stone; compared to the time spent with his new mentor, school was boring and trivial. As a result, William dropped out of school during his junior year.

Off to War

William Faulkner, like many young men of his generation, was determined to take part in World War I, which was then raging in Europe. Despite his parents' opposition, he tried to enlist in the army as an aviator, only to be rejected because he was underweight. Relying on his ability to weave a convincing story, Faulkner then enlisted in the Canadian Royal Air Force (RAF), telling recruiters that his name was William *Faulkner*, that he was British by birth, and that his mother was living in Oxford, Mississippi. (He said nothing to the recruiters about his father.)

Accepted into the RAF's training program, Faulkner continued telling stories, including that he was a student at Yale. Likewise, in letters home he wrote that he had successfully completed the ground school portion of his training and that he had completed a solo flight—both contentions were untrue. Faulkner dreamed of accomplishing these things, but World War I ended before he could earn his wings.

Faced with having to return home without the glorious ac-

Faulkner used his storytelling talents in an attempt to become a World War I aviator.

complishments he had dreamed of, Faulkner hit on an alternative plan: He decided to make up stories about his war experiences. He arrived back in Oxford sporting a mustache, an English lieutenant's uniform, and a limp that he claimed was the result of an airplane crash. Although Faulkner's entire story was a fabrication, he told it so convincingly that he was treated with respect by the people of Oxford.

Writing Efforts

Once Faulkner had settled back into life in Oxford, the twenty-one-year-old resumed his studies with Phil Stone and returned to writing poetry. Pressured by his father, Faulkner eventually enrolled at the University of Mississippi; although he had not graduated from high school, he could take classes as long as he did not declare himself a candidate for a college degree. He rarely attended classes, however. Faulkner's father was unimpressed by his oldest son's performance; similarly, Faulkner's uncle, John Falkner, was direct in his assessment: "That damn Billy is not worth a Mississippi goddamn. Won't hold a job; won't try; won't do anything! He's a Falkner and I hate to say it about my own nephew, but, hell, there's a black sheep in everybody's family and Bill's ours."[35]

Faulkner's interests lay elsewhere, though. He was steadily writing poetry, although only one of his poems had been published. Faulkner longed to leave Oxford and try to sell some of his poetry in New York. He made a brief foray to New York, where he failed to find any buyers for his poems. While in New York, he drank copious amounts of alcohol and briefly worked in a bookstore. The trip was a failure in every way but one: The bookstore's manager, Elizabeth Prall, would be a valuable link to someone in a position to help his career along.

After only a few months, Faulkner returned to Oxford, where his friend Phil Stone found him a job as the postmaster of the University of Mississippi. Faulkner was, however, a failure as postmaster. In 1924 he resigned after he was disciplined by the postal inspector for mismanagement and misconduct. His response was one of immense relief: "Thank God I won't ever again have to be at the beck and call of every son of a bitch who's got two cents to buy a stamp."[36]

A New Friend

Freed from what he saw as the drudgery of working at an everyday job, Faulkner was ready to concentrate all of his energies on his writing. He recognized that one way to hone his craft was to associate with established writers. Faulkner had become a great admirer

of Sherwood Anderson after reading his collection of short stories, titled *Horses and Men*. When he expressed an interest in meeting Anderson, a friend told him that his former boss, Elizabeth Prall, was now married to Anderson. Prall agreed to introduce Faulkner to her husband. In January 1925 Faulkner headed for New Orleans, where the famous author lived.

Faulkner admired the work of author Sherwood Anderson (pictured).

The meeting with Anderson went far better than Faulkner had hoped. It turned out that Anderson came from a background similar to Faulkner's: a small town populated by people with narrow minds and limited aspirations. Unfortunately, though, Faulkner and Anderson also shared another trait: Both men liked to drink—a lot. The two immediately struck up a friendship.

A Try as a Novelist

Faulkner stayed in New Orleans only a short while and then returned briefly to Oxford. During his next visit to New Orleans, he decided to stay in the city, first as a guest of the Andersons and then by renting a small room of his own.

Faulkner had ambitious plans. Rather than be a poet, he now felt it was time to try his hand at novel writing. His first novel, *Soldier's Pay*, attracted the attention of the publisher Boni and Liveright, mostly on the strength of a recommendation from Sherwood Anderson.

Soldier's Pay, which is the story of an aviator wounded in World War I, received respectable reviews. The explicit depictions of sex in the novel made it controversial, however, since most writers up to Faulkner's time shied away from sexual themes or only hinted at sex in vague terms. Even the University of Mississippi refused to accept a copy of the book. Faulkner's own mother, upon reading the book, advised him to leave the country, saying the book was a disgrace.

If measured by the income the book generated, Faulkner's first novel was only a modest success. By the beginning of 1927, he was again broke and living with his parents in Oxford. In his room, he worked on some short stories set in small-town Mississippi. The characters in these stories were based on the people with whom he had grown up: The Snopeses were thinly veiled look-alikes for the rednecks that Faulkner and Phil Stone had joked about years earlier. The other story dealt with a family of Southern gentry, the Sartorises, who closely resembled Faulkner's own kinsmen.

As Faulkner worked at his stories, he realized that he had far more to say than could be contained in shorter works. The story about the Sartoris clan, in particular, demanded a telling in a full-length novel. Titled *Flags in the Dust*, Faulkner was convinced that this was the work that would make him famous. He proudly sent the manuscript off to his editor at Boni and Liveright. The novel was rejected, however—not just by Boni and Liveright but also by every publisher who looked at it, despite several extensive revisions. Devastated, Faulkner could only respond by withdrawing from those around him, and by immersing himself in a new work. This one would not just be a success, it would make Faulkner famous.

The Lyceum building on the University of Mississippi campus. Faulkner's first novel, Soldier's Pay, *was rejected by the university because of its sexual themes.*

The Sound and the Fury

The story Faulkner wrote began as a novella but gradually grew into a full-length novel in four parts. In it, Faulkner tells the tale of an old southern family, the Compsons. As Stephen B. Oates writes, "Here in the Compsons was a dark and compelling tale about the moral impotence of the old established southern families in the modern South, about their aimlessness and sense of doom."[37] Faulkner, on the advice of Phil Stone, titled the novel *The Sound and the Fury*.

As Faulkner was making the final revisions to his new novel, he received surprising and wonderful news: Harcourt Brace and Company, one of the most respected publishing houses in the nation, had agreed to publish *Flags in the Dust*. Although Faulkner was reluctant to take the advice of the editor, Hal Smith, and shorten the novel substantially, he signed the contract he was offered. He also convinced Smith to consider publishing *The Sound and the Fury* as well.

Faulkner did not think *The Sound and the Fury* would have much appeal to the reading public, and therefore did not really expect Harcourt Brace to be interested in the novel. He was right. In January 1929 he received a letter from Alfred Harcourt, who rejected the novel because he did not think it would be profitable. Hal Smith, however, believed in Faulkner's work. He had decided to form his own publishing company, and he offered Faulkner a two-hundred-dollar advance against royalties for the dark tale of southern decay. The money, of course, would not go far, and Faulkner was becoming discouraged, wondering if he would ever be successful as a writer. According to Oates, Faulkner told Phil Stone that "he didn't know why he kept writing—maybe just to stay out of regular work."[38]

Estelle

With *The Sound and the Fury* under contract, Faulkner returned to Oxford, where he spent time writing and pursuing a relationship with his old girlfriend, Estelle Oldham. For years Faulkner had worshiped Oldham from a distance, but when she returned to Oxford following the breakup of her marriage, Faulkner renewed their friendship. He spent as much time as he could with Oldham, even baby-sitting her two children, Malcolm and Cho-Cho, when she had to run errands.

Faulkner had few prospects of being able to support himself—much less Oldham and her two children—and he was uncertain whether he should marry her. But Oldham persisted, and eventually Faulkner agreed to marriage. On June 20, 1929, while Oldham waited outside in the car, Faulkner walked into her father's office and announced his intentions. Then, as Oates explains, "Faulkner marched out to the car and drove Estelle, dainty and happy in her wedding dress, to College Hill Presbyterian Church, where he took her as his wife, with no hope that his art would ever support them."[39]

It was not long before Estelle Faulkner began to see the flaws in her new husband's character. He often went around unshaven and wearing dirty clothes; just as irritating, Faulkner was often uncommunicative. The final step in the publication of *The Sound and the Fury*, reading the galley proof, was at hand, and Faulkner was obsessed with that task. While he worked, he tolerated no interruptions from his bride. Biographer Oates writes, "Without open communication between them, they both drank too much: Faulkner when he wasn't writing, Estelle when he was."[40]

At Rowan Oak

By late 1929 it appeared that Faulkner's writing was going well. Several magazines bought short stories he had written, paying him more than he had earned in royalties from any of the novels he had

Estelle and William Faulkner walk outside their Rowan Oak house. Estelle soon became irritated with William's unkempt appearance and his tendency to be uncommunicative.

published so far. With some money coming in, Faulkner was determined to buy a house for Estelle. This was a bad time to be taking on such a commitment, however. The stock market had just crashed, leading to a nationwide downturn that was to become the Great Depression.

The difficult economic conditions worked to Faulkner's advantage, and he was able to persuade the owner of a run-down antebellum home to sell it to him with no down payment and at a favorable interest rate. Faulkner called his home Rowan Oak, after a type of tree that was a symbol of peace and security to people of Scottish heritage.

Estelle hated Rowan Oak from the beginning. She was used to living well: Her former husband had been wealthy, and she was unimpressed by a house that lacked electricity, water, or indoor plumbing. Faulkner made the best of the situation, however. He hired handymen to help him renovate the old house; when he was not working on the house or on the accompanying gardens, he worked on his writing. In the evenings, Estelle would join her husband on the front porch, where they would each have a glass of bourbon.

Alabama

In spite of her dislike of Rowan Oak, Estelle tried to please Faulkner. Although Estelle's children lived with them, Faulkner wanted children of his own, so although Estelle had been warned that she was too frail to have another child, she ignored this advice. In January 1931, two months ahead of schedule, Estelle and William Faulkner became parents of a baby girl, whom they named Alabama. The child had very little chance of surviving, however. Just ten days after birth, while lying in her bassinet, little Alabama suddenly stopped breathing. Faulkner called the doctor, who informed him that there was nothing to be done for the baby. Faulkner could not do anything either, and Alabama died, leaving her father and mother grief stricken.

Faulkner responded to the loss of his daughter in a time-honored fashion: He immersed himself in his work. He began a new novel, *Light in August*. The popularity of Faulkner's 1931 novel *Sanctuary*, a book about rape and murder in a fictional Mississippi town, had caused several major publishing houses to take interest in him: While he was on a visit to New York, Alfred A. Knopf, Random House, and Viking all tried to convince him to write for them. It seemed at last as though Faulkner would be able to reliably support himself and his family by writing.

Hollywood

Light in August was finished early in 1932. Like most of his previous novels, this one showed no signs of earning him the kind of money he desperately needed just to support himself and his family. Faced with expenses for the upkeep of Rowan Oak, the need to pay taxes on the place, and the demands of creditors, Faulkner took a job that his friend Ben Wasson had lined up for him as a screenwriter for Metro-Goldwyn-Mayer (MGM).

Movie director Howard Hawks (pictured) highly regarded Faulkner's work and helped show him how to write screenplays.

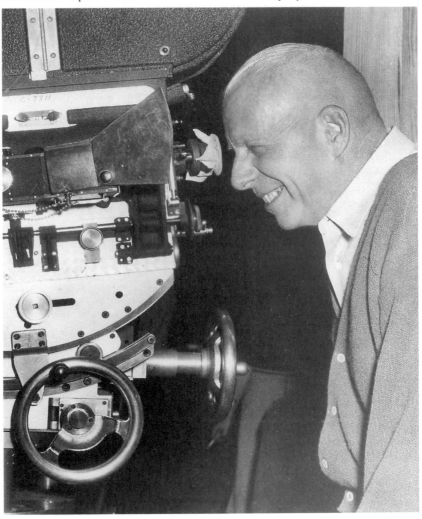

Working in Hollywood repelled Faulkner, but he needed the money. Fortunately for him, a well-regarded movie director, Howard Hawks, had read his work and saw merit in it. Hawks took Faulkner under his wing and showed him how writing screenplays differed from writing novels, thus helping Faulkner make the transition to this new literary form.

Faulkner's new career led to other changes as well. His relationship with Estelle, which had been troubled from the beginning, had grown ever more remote. The birth of a second child, Jill, had pleased Faulkner greatly, but Estelle's dislike of Faulkner's sullen silences and his resentment of what he saw as her extravagant spending habits had left the marriage an empty shell. When, in December 1935, Faulkner met Meta Carpenter, a secretary working in Howard Hawks's office, he was immediately attracted to her. Although Carpenter spurned his initial advances, she eventually responded to his charm, and they began an extended affair.

Other aspects of Faulkner's life did not change during this period, though. He kept drinking heavily, with only brief periods of sobriety. Faulkner was also dividing his time between Mississippi and California, between Estelle and Meta Carpenter, and between his novels and screenwriting.

When he was not working on screenplays, Faulkner was laboring to complete another novel, *Absalom, Absalom!* The work had been going slowly, but by early 1936 he had completed the first draft. While trying to finish the novel, Faulkner had kept his drinking in check. With the main work completed, however, his alcoholism took over; the binge that followed was so severe that his family placed him in a sanitarium about fifty miles from Oxford to dry out.

Faulkner felt himself pulled in different directions, both personally and professionally. He hated Hollywood because of the constant motion that seemed a part of life there, and because of the snobbishness of many of the people in the movie business. Yet, he knew that his novels alone were not earning him the money he needed. In addition, he loved Meta Carpenter but could not bear to divorce Estelle.

During this time Estelle was drinking heavily, too. Although his two stepchildren were old enough to look after themselves, Faulkner was worried that his wife was not caring properly for Jill while he was away in Hollywood. In order to keep an eye on his daughter, Faulkner decided to take both Estelle and Jill with him when he returned to the West Coast in August 1936.

The move strained Faulkner's relationship with Carpenter. Though he tried to reassure her by speaking in general terms of divorcing Estelle, Faulkner made no concrete moves in that direction.

Convinced that Faulkner would never actually divorce Estelle, Carpenter married a wealthy concert pianist she had met, Wolfgang Rebner. As the date of her wedding approached in the spring of 1937, Faulkner responded by drinking still more. He was unable to give up his love for Meta, and went so far as to try to see her and Rebner socially—anything to allow him to spend time with her. On one occasion, during an extended visit to New York, Faulkner made a dinner date with the couple. But he got drunk before the scheduled meeting, and in a stupor he fell against a hot steam pipe in his hotel bathroom, burning himself so badly that he needed medical treatment. Meta and her husband came to his bedside, where Faulkner confessed his resolve to keep loving her: "Meta, one of my characters has said, 'between grief and nothing I will take grief.'"[41]

Recognition

Faulkner's luck—in terms of his work—changed for the better in early 1938. The film rights for one of his novels, *The Unvanquished*, unexpectedly sold to MGM for twenty-five thousand dollars; Faulkner's share of the proceeds was nineteen thousand dollars. Determined to invest this money wisely, Faulkner bought a large farm outside of Oxford, which he named Greenfield Farm. He installed his brother, John, to manage the place for him.

His luck improved still more the following year. In January 1939 Faulkner was elected to the National Institute of Arts and Letters. And later that same year his short story "Barn Burning" won the O. Henry Memorial Award for the best short story of 1939.

The good times did not last. Needing money, Faulkner returned to Hollywood in 1942 and 1943, where he knew that he could at least earn enough money to keep himself alive. One of his assignments turned out to be writing a screenplay based on Ernest Hemingway's novel, *To Have and Have Not*. The director of the film, Howard Hawks, had paid Faulkner quite a compliment: When Hemingway scoffed that the novel was not suitable for a movie, Hawks told him, "I'll get Faulkner to do it. He can write better than you can anyway."[42]

Intruder in the Dust

By 1945 Faulkner realized that he had not managed to complete an original novel in ten years. He continued to try to complete a new work, however, and by the spring of 1948 he had finished work on *Intruder in the Dust*. The novel, which is about the relationship between a southern black farmer and a white teenager who refuses to go along with the racial prejudice of the South, brought Faulkner what he needed most: money. His share of the movie rights came to forty thousand dollars.

The change in Faulkner's fortunes was reflected in the critical response to his work. Late in the fall of 1948 he learned that he had been elected to the American Academy of Arts and Letters, a highly select subset of the National Institute, of which he was already a member. Then, in late April 1950, the academy awarded him the William Dean Howells Medal, which is only awarded once every five years to one writer, in recognition of the excellence of the fiction he or she has produced during that time. Even greater recognition was soon to come, however.

The Nobel Prize

In November 1950 Faulkner received a call from a Swedish news reporter, telling him that he had just been awarded the 1949 Nobel Prize for literature. As word spread around Oxford, Faulkner's fellow townspeople were astonished. One local resident, when told the news, said, "I guess he's appreciated a whole lot more outside than he is around here."[43]

Faulkner at first declined to travel to Stockholm to attend the Nobel award ceremonies. Under pressure from Estelle, however, he agreed to go, partly because he was told that his daughter, Jill, could accompany him and that the trip would mean a lot to her. Right up to the moment that Faulkner received his award from the king of Sweden, there was doubt that he would manage to get through the ceremony because he so dreaded speaking in public. The speech he gave, however, was an eloquent tribute to the role of the writer in the modern world:

> It is easy enough to say that man is immortal simply because he will endure: that when the last ding-dong of doom has clanged and faded from the last worthless rock hanging tideless in the last red and dying evening, that even then there will still be one more sound: that of his

puny inexhaustible voice, still talking. I refuse to accept this. I believe that man will not merely endure: he will prevail. He is immortal, not because he alone among creatures has an inexhaustible voice, but because he has a soul, a spirit capable of compassion and sacrifice and endurance. The poet's, the writer's, duty is to write about these things. It is his privilege to help man endure by lifting his heart, by reminding him of the courage and honor and hope and pride and compassion and pity and sacrifice which have been the glory of his past. The poet's voice need not merely be the record of man, it can be one of the props, the pillars to help him endure and prevail.[44]

Faulkner and his daughter board a plane, beginning their trip to Stockholm for the Nobel Prize ceremony.

Continuing Problems

Faulkner continued to work on a novel that he had been tinkering with for years, but the process was extraordinarily difficult for him, primarily because the setting, France during World War I, was so unfamiliar to him. He finally did complete the novel, titled *A Fable*. That book, a fanciful tale about a French soldier who starts a mutiny during World War I, earned him the Pulitzer Prize.

Fame did nothing to cure Faulkner's drinking, though. Receiving the Nobel and Pulitzer Prizes punctuated hospital stays to treat the effects of his alcoholism.

Despite his problems, Faulkner stayed active in the world of letters. He participated in the U.S. government's People to People Program, which was designed to introduce people in the Soviet Union to American culture. Likewise, Faulkner accepted an offer to become writer-in-residence at the University of Virginia.

During this time, one of Faulkner's major worries was eventually put to rest. The acclaim that flowed from being a Nobel laureate caused his books to sell to the reading public, and the royalties were finally amounting to something. He had now written eighteen novels. In the spring of 1961, he started on another novel, and finished it in just a few months. *The Reivers* was to be his last novel.

Eternal Tomorrow

By July 1962 Faulkner was suffering from intense pain. He had experienced a couple of bad falls off of his horse in the preceding months, injuring his back on both occasions. Over the Fourth of July, he went on yet another drinking binge, this time mixing painkillers and tranquilizers with bourbon. Once again his wife and nephew placed him in a sanitarium on July 5 in hopes of curing him of his alcoholism.

Shortly after arrival in the sanitarium, Faulkner complained of chest pains. Sometime in the early morning hours of July 6, William Faulkner died. He was sixty-five years old. At his funeral a day later, his brother, John, spoke to the people assembled by the graveside: "He has stepped into an eternal tomorrow that has left him forever in Yoknapatawpha County. He can never leave us again."[45]

CHAPTER 5

James Baldwin: Victory over Silence

As a poet, essayist, and novelist, James Baldwin worked to expose the sorrows that haunted the lives of African Americans. Baldwin became one of the most respected writers of the 1940s, 1950s, and 1960s.

James Arthur Jones was born in Harlem in New York City on August 2, 1924, to Emma Berdis Jones. James's biological father was not a part of his life or his mother's, so young James was officially considered "illegitimate." But Emma did not allow that condition to last for long; within three years she was married to

In his writings, poet, essayist, and novelist James Baldwin described the sorrows that permeated the lives of African Americans.

David Baldwin, and her son took his stepfather's last name. David Baldwin already had one son by a previous marriage, and over the years, the Baldwin family grew steadily. Eventually, James had eight siblings, and he was expected to help look after the younger ones.

Life in Harlem during the 1920s and 1930s was difficult for the Baldwins. The Great Depression was on, so David Baldwin's job as a factory worker paid little, and the cost of living was higher in Harlem than in other parts of New York City. Housing was crowded and of poor quality, and the streets were dangerous places where crime was common.

David Baldwin responded to the dangers of the streets by keeping James and his siblings indoors as much as he could, which limited their ability to make friends. Inside the family's apartment, Baldwin's word was law, and he punished his children with beatings for even small infractions.

Aspiring Writer

In addition to his job as a factory worker, James's father was a part-time Pentacostal preacher. His mother was also a devout Christian. It was natural, then, for James to aspire to be a preacher. He did not stay long with his boyhood religion, however, and by the time he was seventeen, he had left the church behind. The influence of his Christian upbringing was lasting, though. In the words of biographer James Campbell, "The prophesy of wrath and the quest for salvation shaped his imagination, just as the vocabulary and cadence of the King James Bible and the rhetoric of the pulpit were at the heart of his literary style."[46]

David Baldwin discouraged his children from any reading except from the Bible. Despite his stepfather's attitude, James grew up a reader. He was encouraged to read by his mother and by one of his early teachers, Orilla Miller. His reading, in turn, helped him develop into a skilled writer. James, in turn, made an impact on those who taught him. Another teacher, this one at the junior high school James attended, later recalled that he could write "better than anyone in the school—from the principal on down."[47]

The first person of importance to James as a writer, ironically, was a painter named Beauford Delaney. Years later, James would recall that their friendship helped him develop his powers of observation: "I learned about light. . . . He is seeing all the time; and the reality of his *seeing* caused me to begin to see."[48]

Even as a teenager, James knew where he was headed. In his high school's yearbook, Baldwin's stated goal was to become a novelist and a playwright. It would not be long before his dream would come true.

Gaining a Mentor

After graduating from high school in the summer of 1941, however, Baldwin was headed down a far different path. He had intended to go to college, but as the oldest child in his family, he was expected to get a job and help support his parents and eight younger siblings. At the time, the only job he could find was as a laborer, so Baldwin went to work laying railroad tracks. This was just one of a number of dead-end jobs that he would hold over the next few years.

David Baldwin's health had been failing, and barely two years after his son graduated from high school, the elder man died, leaving his wife and nine children deep in poverty. The loss of his stepfather meant that James was compelled to become the head of this large household.

Despite the difficulty of trying to support his family on his laborer's wages, Baldwin kept working at writing a novel. Meant to be autobiographical, the novel was tentatively titled

Baldwin introduced himself to the man who became his mentor, writer Richard Wright (pictured).

Crying Holy. Because he had been deeply moved by the work of the famous African American writer Richard Wright, Baldwin sought Wright out at his home, book in hand, and introduced himself.

Wright liked the material that Baldwin had shown him and helped the inexperienced writer obtain his first monetary support for his writing. Thanks to Wright's influence, Baldwin obtained a five-hundred-dollar grant from the Eugene F. Saxton Memorial Trust, a fund that gave monetary grants to aspiring writers.

With the money from the grant, Baldwin was able to support himself while he worked to complete *Crying Holy*. He was not, however, successful in getting the work published. Three different publishers turned the manuscript down. He did have one modest success, though: A book review he had written was published by the *Nation*, as was a second review he wrote. Baldwin was only twenty-two, but he found himself at least being taken seriously as a literary critic, if not as a novelist.

A Matter of Identity

In just a few years Baldwin had to say good-bye to his mentor—at least temporarily. Fed up with the overt racism of 1940s America, Wright moved to France in 1947. Baldwin had also experienced racism, and he, too, longed to go to France.

In addition to losing Wright, Baldwin also was forced, as he left his teen years behind, to come to terms with another aspect of his identity: his homosexuality. Baldwin dealt with racism and his own sexuality in much the same way. In the words of biographer James Campbell, "Baldwin had grown up to the shocking discovery that the colour of his skin stood between him and the possibility of life lived to its full potential—between him and life itself, in fact. He made up his mind not to allow his sexual orientation to fortify the barrier."[49]

To France

In 1948, not long after he had begun to be recognized for his critical talents, Baldwin decided to go to France. He knew that by going abroad he would be losing out on chances to write literary criticism, but there were other advantages, as biographer W. J. Weatherby notes: "Most of [the various editors he had worked with] were vaguely encouraging. After all he was following a well-trod literary trail. It was too far away to send many books to be reviewed, but as an American—a black American—in Europe, the experience was bound to give him new subjects for essays."[50]

Baldwin was only able to go because he had received another monetary grant, this time for fifteen hundred dollars from a philanthropist named Julius Rosenwald. Baldwin arrived in Paris essentially broke: After giving some of the grant money to his mother and siblings and spending nearly the rest on his passage to Europe, Baldwin was left with only forty dollars.

Philanthropist Julius Rosenwald's grant enabled Baldwin to travel to France.

The first thing that Baldwin did upon his arrival in Paris was to renew his friendship with Richard Wright. The older writer introduced Baldwin to another American who provided the young newcomer with his first writing assignment: an essay for the new literary magazine *Zero*. Unfortunately, the essay was to be the wedge that opened a gulf between Baldwin and Wright. Titled "Everybody's Protest Novel," the essay offended Wright when Baldwin compared his mentor's work with Harriet Beecher Stowe's *Uncle Tom's Cabin*, which Baldwin criticized heavily. The offense Wright took at this essay surprised Baldwin. Later, Baldwin recalled, "It simply had not occurred to me that the essay could be interpreted [as an attack on Richard Wright]"[51] Although Baldwin had not meant to offend Wright, the damage to their friendship was done, and the two would have an uncomfortable professional relationship from then on.

Lucien

Not long after his arrival in Paris, Baldwin met someone who would become a significant presence in his life for many years to come. Lucien Happersberger was a seventeen-year-old Swiss youth who befriended Baldwin. That relationship was far more complex than mere friendship, however. Baldwin's biographer notes, "Baldwin accepted Lucien first as a friend, then as a younger brother, and then as a lover. But Happersberger insists that the first of those was the main nourishment of their relationship."[52]

Paris was a place where Baldwin could do almost anything he wanted: He could find good conversation, and he could always find someone who would buy him a drink. With all the distractions that Paris offered, Baldwin had trouble finding the time he needed to work on the novel that had been nagging him. Fortunately, Happersberger provided the solution: His parents owned a chalet in the Alps, and he and Baldwin were allowed to spend the

Surrounded by the distractions of Paris, including this café where he occasionally ate, Baldwin found it difficult to concentrate on writing.

winter of 1951–1952 there. It was in this mountain hideaway that Baldwin was finally able to finish his first novel, which explores the religious conversion experience of a fourteen-year-old boy. Although Baldwin had originally titled the work *Crying Holy*, he renamed the finished book *Go Tell It on the Mountain*.

A Book with Some Promise

Baldwin's agent submitted the completed manuscript to the well-respected publishing firm Alfred A. Knopf, where it found an admiring audience with William Rossa Cole, who in addition to being the firm's publicity director was also a part-time editor. Others at the company, such as editor Arthur Ogden, were not as certain of the novel's quality; in fact, editor-in-chief Harold Strauss very nearly rejected the manuscript entirely. Fortunately for Baldwin, yet another editor, Philip Vaudrin thought the book was promising. Vaudrin gave the young author $250 and promised him another $750 once he had revised the manuscript to the point where Knopf could publish it.

When *Go Tell It on the Mountain* was published in May 1953, it was widely praised. But in spite of the novel's success, Baldwin could not feel completely at home in the literary world he inhabited. He wrote an essay titled "Stranger in the Village" in which he used his life in the Swiss village where Lucien's chalet was located as a metaphor for the difficulties he was experiencing as an African

American writer trying to establish himself among whites. In his essay, Baldwin writes, "The most illiterate [of the villagers] is related, in a way that I am not, to Dante, Shakespeare, Michelangelo. . . . Go back a few centuries and they are in their full glory—but I am in Africa, watching the conquerors arrive."[53]

The Amen Corner

Baldwin returned to New York to get *Go Tell It on the Mountain* accepted and published, but he did not stay any longer than necessary. The year after it was published, he returned to Europe. He tried to work on a couple of stories and several book projects, but he abandoned all of these. Eventually, however, he wrote the play *The Amen Corner*, which, like his novel, incorporates themes that were likely based on Baldwin's experiences as the son of a preacher.

Watching his talented new author take time to write a play did not please Baldwin's editor at Knopf, who was hoping that Baldwin would write another novel for him. Baldwin was working on a novel, but he also wanted to assemble some of his previously published essays into a book. This collection, titled *Notes of a Native Son*, helped introduce Baldwin's nonfiction to a wider audience than just those people who subscribed to the magazines that had originally published his essays.

Baldwin eventually did as his editor hoped and began working on a second novel. After several title changes, Balwin settled on *Giovanni's Room*. Published in 1956, *Giovanni's Room* was so controversial that Knopf refused to publish it. In the novel, Baldwin portrays sexual relations between two gay men, and Knopf's editors feared that the book might be banned as pornography if it were published as Baldwin had submitted it.

It turned out that Knopf's fears were baseless: The novel was published first in Britain and then in the United States by Dial Press. Because homosexuality was a taboo subject for writers in the 1950s, *Giovanni's Room* was not universally well received by critics. Some reviewers, though, did praise Baldwin's new novel because he treated his subject in a sensitive manner. In any case, Baldwin's reputation as an up-and-coming writer was assured.

Personal Insecurity

Baldwin was on the move in his chosen profession. Three books of his had been published—*Go Tell It on the Mountain*, *Notes of a Native Son*, and *Giovanni's Room*—and each was well regarded by most critics. It was a different story in Baldwin's personal life, however. Although he had found happiness with Lucien, their alliance

Segregation and other injustices influenced Baldwin to write about an African American's struggle for identity.

did not develop into a committed long-term relationship. As biographer Campbell tells it,

> [Baldwin] was sensitive about being small and not terribly handsome; certain that people were going to leave him anyway, his instinct was to push and push, to see how much they would take before they did. He felt orphaned in Europe; he was depressed at his failure to create a stable, lasting relationship, and aware that even if he did succeed, it would be a union without children.[54]

Not only was Baldwin unhappy with his personal life, he was also distressed by the fact that living overseas meant that he could not participate in the rapidly growing civil rights movement in America. He knew that he should be home—but knowing where his home really was eluded him. In the end he knew he must return to America, and in July 1957 he arrived in New York. Again, he did not stay there long; but when he left, it was not for Europe, but for the American South.

Baldwin observed the strife occurring on a daily basis as southern blacks protested against the traditions and laws that made segregation a way of life all over America, but particularly in the South. By now a highly experienced writer, Baldwin wrote movingly of what he saw. Rather than expressing the conflict between whites and blacks as a struggle for political power, though, Baldwin depicted it as a struggle for identity. That struggle had been going on since before the Civil War. As he wrote in a later book,

> "Perhaps the master who had coupled [had intercourse] with his slave saw the guilt in his wife's pale eyes in the morning. And the wife saw his children in the slave quarters, saw the way his concubine, the sensual-looking black girl, looked at her—a woman after all, and scarcely less sensual, but white. . . . And the white man must have seen his guilt written somewhere else, seen it all the time, even if his sin was merely lust, even if his sin lay in nothing but his power: in the eyes of the black man."[55]

"What You Want, Boy?"

Baldwin quickly learned that in the American South, the fact that he was a well-regarded author mattered less to whites than the fact that he was black. Later, in his autobiography *No Name in the Street*, Baldwin recalled an incident that occurred when he entered a restaurant in Montgomery, Alabama:

> "I will never forget it. I don't know if I can describe it. . . . Every white face turned to stone: the arrival of the messenger of death could not have had a more devastating effect than the appearance in the restaurant doorway of a small, unarmed, utterly astounded black man. I had realized my error as soon as I opened the door: but the absolute terror on all these white faces—I swear that not a soul moved—paralyzed me. They stared at me, I stared at them.
>
> The spell was broken by one of those women, produced, I hope, only in the South, with a face like a rusty hatchet, and eyes like two rusty nails—nails left from the crucifixion. She rushed at me as though to club me down, and she barked—for it was not a human sound: 'what you want, boy? What you want in here?'"[56]

Many of Baldwin's observations are included in the collection *Nobody Knows My Name: More Notes of a Native Son*, which was published in 1961. The book was an instant success and made Baldwin a celebrity. But despite his new fame, Baldwin remained restless. He continued to travel, never staying in one place for very long.

The Fire Next Time

Baldwin's travels in the early 1960s had included brief visits to Chicago, where he met with Elijah Muhammad, the leader of the Nation of Islam, or, as the group was popularly known, the Black Muslims. Baldwin was of two minds about Muhammad and his message of black separatism. On the one hand, Baldwin was charmed by Muhammad, who somewhat reminded him of his stepfather. As biographer W. J. Weatherby describes the meeting, "Baldwin wondered if [Elijah Muhammad] would be as angry and bitter as his stepfather. . . . [But he] made Baldwin think of his stepfather as he might have been 'if we had been friends.'"[57] The meeting with Elijah Muhammad led to a commission from the magazine *Commentary* to write an article on the Black Muslims. This article, originally titled "Down at the Cross," would eventually appear paired with another shorter work as the book, *The Fire Next Time*.

During the 1960s, Baldwin visited Chicago and met with Elijah Muhammad (pictured), the leader of the Nation of Islam and advocate of black separatism.

The early 1960s were a productive time for Baldwin. Not only did he make a start on "Down at the Cross," which was to make him internationally famous, but he also completed work on a novel that he had been working on for several years, *Another Country*. The novel was bound to be controversial. It dealt with a number of topics that were sensitive at the time, including heterosexual and homosexual sex and race relations. Unlike his previous books, however, this one was not well received by the critics. Some called it pornographic; others simply dismissed it as poorly written. Baldwin was able to take some comfort, however, in the fact that, despite the poor reviews (or perhaps because of some of them), the novel became a best-seller.

The lengthy essay that came to be titled "The Fire Next Time" was published in the *New Yorker* in November 1962 as "Letter from a Region of My Mind." With the publication of this essay and the later book that contained it, Baldwin came to be regarded as a major critic of race relations in America. In this role, Baldwin soon found himself meeting with one of the most influential men in America: Robert F. Kennedy, who was the U.S. attorney general and the brother of President John F. Kennedy.

Unfortunately, Baldwin's relations with Kennedy quickly soured. During a meeting on race relations that had been arranged by Kennedy and was attended by a number of black artists and writers, Baldwin commented,

> "You do not understand [the situation of black Americans] at all. Your grandfather came as an immigrant from Ireland and your brother is president of the United States. Generations before your family came as immigrants, my ancestors came to this country in chains, as slaves. We are still required to supplicate and beg you for justice and decency."[58]

The attorney general was insulted by Baldwin's directness. Kennedy, in his role as the nation's top law enforcement officer, saw to it that the FBI kept a close watch on Baldwin.

The Price of Fame

Baldwin was famous now. He even complained to an interviewer that he could no longer go to his favorite bars in New York because he would be instantly recognized. At one point, he remarked, "I'm probably the most photographed writer in the world."[59]

The fame and the attention were distractions that affected his next major book, *Tell Me How Long the Train's Been Gone*, a semi-autobiographical novel about a writer who escapes the Harlem ghetto. The novel was criticized because Baldwin had failed to exert enough control over both its structure and its characters. Moreover, many white readers were offended by what seemed to them a strident, critical tone when the author described most of the white characters.

Despite the seeming career decline, Baldwin continued to work at his craft, publishing seven books between 1971 and 1976. Whatever the state of his professional health, however, his physical health was becoming precarious. The regimen of late nights, alcohol, and too many cigarettes was taking its toll. In early 1971 he suffered a physical collapse while staying in Paris. After a stay in the American hospital there, he moved to an agreeable little town, Saint-Paul, near the French Riviera city of Nice, and settled into a lengthy convalescence.

Just Above My Head

Baldwin's publisher, Dial Press, had been hounding him to write another lengthy novel—one that would return him to the kind of fame he had generated when *Another Country* was published. The author tried to deliver by writing *Just Above My Head*, a six-hundred-page novel about a gay gospel singer and a fashion model. Biographer James Campbell, however, points out the work's flaws:

> The defects inherent in all his novels, with the exception of *Go Tell It on the Mountain*, were again plain to see in the new one: too many bloodless characters, too neatly divided into goodies and baddies; too strong a dependence on colour as an indicator of virtue; . . . too many rambling conversations and descriptions . . . too many rhetorical passages which belong not to the narrator but to James Baldwin.[60]

The early 1980s found Baldwin working on several projects at once, each from a different literary genre: a novel, *No Papers for Mohammed*, a play, *The Welcome Table*, and a collective biography *Remember This House*. Of these projects, the only one he finished was *The Welcome Table*, and none gained much attention in literary circles.

"He Ain't Heavy"

By the middle of the 1980s, Baldwin's lifestyle was catching up to him. For years a smoker and a drinker, he had to have an operation for cancer of the esophagus that proved unsuccessful, and the disease invaded his liver. Gradually, Baldwin weakened to the point that he could no longer walk. His younger brother David had to carry him

Baldwin gets off of a plane after touring Europe with his stage play, The Amen Corner. *His works inspired other African American writers.*

from his bedroom to the dinner table. Baldwin said to his brother, "That old song ain't no lie." When asked what song he was referring to, Baldwin replied, "He ain't heavy, he's my brother."[61] James Baldwin's heart gave out, and he died on November 30, 1987.

He was buried in Hartsdale, New York, a suburb of New York City. He left behind a body of works that are rightly admired. But perhaps even more importantly, he paved the way for other African American writers. Three of the best-known black writers of the late twentieth century, novelist Toni Morrison, poet and playwright Amiri Baraka, and poet Maya Angelou have credited Baldwin with inspiring their work. Baldwin's books continue to be available to readers in libraries and sold in bookstores, thus inspiring new generations of writers.

CHAPTER 6

Flannery O'Connor: The Voice of Southern Gothic

Flannery O'Connor has always been a puzzle to those who study American literature. She was raised a Roman Catholic, and throughout her life she remained devoted to her faith. Yet, in her fiction she depicts characters and themes whose grotesqueness seem at odds with that faith. For O'Connor, however, there was no contrast between O'Connor's beliefs and fiction will continue to fascinate readers in decades to come.

Flannery O'Connor, often depicted grotesque characters and themes in her stories.

contradiction. As she once wrote, "My own feeling is that writers who see by the light of their Christian faith will have in these times, the sharpest eyes for the grotesque, for the perverse, and for the unacceptable."[62] The contrast between O'Connor's beliefs and fiction will continue to fascinate readers in decades to come.

In the Minority

Mary Flannery O'Connor was born on March 25, 1925, to Regina and Edward O'Connor Jr. Mary Flannery's father had his own real estate agency, the Dixie Realty Company. Eventually, O'Connor was able to expand his agency's operations into the construction business.

Mary Flannery's parents were devoutly Catholic, which made them a minority among the residents of Savannah, Georgia, who were mostly Protestants. Because Catholics experienced discrimination and harassment at the hands of some bigoted southerners during the 1920s, the O'Connors chose to live in a section of Savannah where other Catholics lived, known as Lafayette Square.

Like many of their neighbors, the O'Connors sent their daughter to the local Catholic school, St. Vincent's Grammar School, which was located near their home. At St. Vincent's, Mary Flannery studied reading, writing, and math, along with her catechism—that is, the basics of the Catholic faith.

As a child Mary Flannery participated in the same sorts of activities many of her schoolmates engaged in. She joined the Girl Scouts, for example, although she did not care for the outdoor activities such as hikes. At home, Mary Flannery showed an interest in animals. She played with ducks and chickens that her family kept in their backyard, and this interest in domestic fowl lasted her entire life.

But Mary Flannery had other interests as well. A solitary child, she showed an early interest in writing. As an eleven-year-old she

A man relaxes by a fountain in Lafayette Square, the section of Savannah where O'Connor was raised.

wrote stories and poetry for her parents. Her father carried samples of his daughter's writing with him, proudly showing them off to his friends.

A Difficult Move

Mary Flannery was only thirteen when, in 1938, finances forced her family to move. Edward O'Connor's business suffered during the Great Depression because few people had the money to buy homes. To make ends meet, O'Connor took a job with the newly created Federal Housing Administration. Appointed as a real estate appraiser for this agency, he had to move to Atlanta, and he took his family with him.

The move did not suit O'Connor's only daughter, however. Mary Flannery and her mother soon relocated to her mother's girlhood home of Milledgeville, Georgia, where Mary Flannery enrolled at Peabody High School. Because of his job, Edward O'Connor remained behind in Atlanta.

Not satisfied with the move to Atlanta, Regina O'Connor and her daughter relocated to Milledgeville, Georgia,(pictured).

Mary Flannery soon displayed her talent as a writer and artist while working for her high school's newspaper, the *Peabody Palladium*. At about this same time, she developed a fondness for the writing of Edgar Allan Poe; in particular, she was attracted to his novel *The Narrative of Arthur Gordon Pym*.

Back in Atlanta O'Connor's father was in ill health. At first, doctors thought he had arthritis, but in 1938 he was diagnosed with lupus, a deadly disorder of the immune system in which the body's disease-fighting apparatus begins attacking its own tissues. The disease had no cure, and on February 1, 1941, when his daughter was only fifteen years old, Edward O'Connor died.

Just Flannery

Just a little over a year after her father's death, O'Connor graduated from high school. She had done well enough in her studies to get into college, and she chose to attend Georgia State College for Women, which was located just a couple of blocks from her home in Milledgeville. It was here that she dropped her first name, signing up for her courses as just Flannery O'Connor (although her family and friends continued to address her as Mary Flannery).

O'Connor continued to be interested in writing, and she majored in both English and sociology. It was at this time that she began writing humorous short works about her two aunts and the college professor who all lived in her mother's home. Two examples of these short prose pieces are "My Relitives" (O'Connor's spelling) and "Why I Chose Heart Trouble."

O'Connor thrived in college. She contributed stories and poems for the college's literary magazine, the *Corinthian*, and eventually became the editor of that publication. In addition, O'Connor worked as the art editor for *The Spectrum*, which was the college's yearbook.

By this time, O'Connor was trying to get some of her work published elsewhere, although with no success. She sent some of the cartoons she drew to the prestigious magazine, the *New Yorker*, but to no avail. She would have to look elsewhere for affirmation of her talent, at least for the moment.

On to Iowa

O'Connor had been applying to graduate schools to continue her English studies, but she needed a scholarship in order to afford it. The University of Iowa offered her full tuition plus a small allowance of sixty-five dollars per term. With this aid, O'Connor could afford to leave Milledgeville behind, although she would continue to write regularly to her mother and keep abreast of events in her hometown.

Flannery O'Connor's first term at Iowa was a huge success. She gained admission to the prestigious Writers' Workshop, where she met such influential literary figures as Robert Penn Warren and Andrew Lytle. In addition, the director of the Writers' Workshop, Paul Engle, encouraged O'Connor to submit some of her short stories to literary magazines such as the *Sewanee Review*.

Hard Going

Despite the encouragement O'Connor received from her mentor at the Writers' Workshop, she soon found that getting published was no easy task. She returned to campus following the Christmas break to find that the two stories she had submitted to the *Sewanee Review* had been rejected. Engle continued to encourage her though, and he advised her to expand her reading of works by established writers such as James Joyce, Franz Kafka, and William Faulkner. On the advice of another faculty member, Paul Horgan, O'Connor began committing a set number of hours each day to uninterrupted writing.

During her second term at Iowa, O'Connor's story "The Geranium" was accepted for publication in the literary journal *Accent*. Another story, "The Coat," was also accepted by another magazine, but O'Connor refused to allow publication unless she was paid, and so the story did not get published.

Hope

Renewed hope that her efforts might bear fruit came as she began her second year at Iowa. The English department offered her a fellowship and gave her a stipend amounting to twenty dollars per month. Better still, Engle brought her work to the attention of John Selby, the editor in chief of the publisher Rinehart and Company.

While her mentor was promoting her short fiction, O'Connor herself was beginning work on a novel. (The work would eventually be published under the title *Wise Blood*, but not for several years.) This new phase in O'Connor's budding career proved to be a good one for her. She submitted the first four chapters to be considered for the Rinehart-Iowa Fiction Award, a competition for first-time novelists, and won the prize of $750. Along with the money was an option from Rinehart and Company to publish the completed novel.

Continuing Study

With the close of the 1946–1947 academic year, O'Connor completed the requirements for a master's degree by submitting her thesis in the form of a collection of her short stories entitled *The Geranium: A Collection of Short Stories*. Rather than leave Iowa, however, O'Connor elected to stay on, this time as a postgraduate student.

O'Connor's efforts as a writer began to pay off monetarily as well. She sold one of the stories from her master's thesis, "The Turkey," to *Mademoiselle* magazine for three hundred dollars, and the *Sewanee Review* bought the opening chapter from her novel, titled "The Train," for just over one hundred dollars.

Yaddo

Other testimony to O'Connor's growing reputation came with an invitation to spend part of the summer of 1948 at Yaddo, an artists' colony located near Saratoga Springs, New York. Such an invitation was a tremendous honor since only those writers and artists considered most promising were asked to spend time in the

In the summer of 1948, O'Connor was invited to stay at Yaddo, a prestigious artists' colony located near Saratoga Springs, New York.

colony. The move to Yaddo proved a turning point in O'Connor's career: Rather than accepting the renewed fellowship that her old mentor at Iowa offered her, she instead chose to return to Yaddo and stay through the end of the year.

While she was at Yaddo, O'Connor decided to pursue other possible publishers for her novel and hired Elizabeth McKee as a literary agent. In her letter to McKee, O'Connor was honest in her characterization of herself and her work, describing herself as someone who worked slowly and methodically:

> I am writing you in my vague and slack season and mainly because I am being impressed just now with the money I am not making by having stories in such places as AMERICAN LETTERS. I am a very slow worker and it is possible that I won't write another story until I finish this novel and that no other chapters of the novel will prove salable.[63]

Even though she had decided to look beyond Rinehart, McKee convinced O'Connor to send the first nine chapters of her novel to John Selby, the editor in chief at Rinehart. Selby was not impressed and wrote to O'Connor, explaining that he was looking for work that was more conventional. O'Connor was irritated by this criticism, and she wrote to her agent, expressing that annoyance:

> The criticism is vague and really tells me nothing except that they don't like it. I feel the objections they raise are connected with its virtues, and the thought of working with them specifically to correct these lacks they mention is repulsive to me. The letter is addressed to a slightly dim-witted Camp-fire Girl, and I cannot look with composure on getting a lifetime of others like them.[64]

"Prematurely Arrogant"

O'Connor's relationship with Selby and Rinehart became increasingly strained. At one point, she wrote to her old mentor, Paul Engle,

> I will not be hurried or directed by Rinehart. I think they are interested in the conventional and I have had no indication that they are very bright. . . . If they don't feel I am worth giving more money to and leaving alone, then they should let me go. . . . Selby and I came to the conclusion that I was "prematurely arrogant." I supplied him with the phrase.[65]

At Yaddo, O'Connor developed a professional relationship with poet Robert Lowell, (left), who helped further her career.

The controversy over her relationship with Selby and Rinehart was both personal and professional, but O'Connor showed herself capable of taking a political stand as well. During her stay at Yaddo, it was revealed that another resident of the colony, Agnes Smedley, had served as an agent for the Soviet Union; as a result, the FBI launched an investigation of the colony and its director, Elizabeth Ames. Hoping to insulate Yaddo from political involvement of this sort, O'Connor joined poet Robert Lowell in demanding the resignation of Ames, who had brought Smedley to Yaddo in the first place. This alliance led to a professional relationship with Lowell, who introduced O'Connor to Robert Giroux, one of the editors at Harcourt Brace and Company.

A Dreaded Diagnosis

O'Connor's relationship with Robert Giroux and Harcourt Brace bore fruit in October 1950 when she received a contract for the publication of *Wise Blood*. The pleasure at having a firm commitment from such a prestigious publishing house was tempered, though, when she began suffering from pains in her arms and shoulders. The doctor she visited told her she was suffering from arthritis. But on her trip to Milledgeville for Christmas, O'Connor became seriously ill. The doctors who examined her there diagnosed her as having rheumatoid arthritis and prescribed doses of cortisone. Further tests, however, would bring far more unwelcome news.

As 1951 opened, O'Connor's doctor in Milledgeville consulted with an internist in Atlanta, Arthur J. Merrill, who suspected that O'Connor was suffering from lupus, the same illness that had killed her father. Further tests, administered at the Emory University Hospital in Atlanta, confirmed that diagnosis. To treat the effects of the disease, O'Connor was given a powerful derivative of cortisone known as adrenocorticotropic hormone (ACTH).

A Published Novelist

O'Connor spent much of the year convalescing on the dairy farm her mother operated outside of Milledgeville. Although weakened by the effects of her ACTH treatments, she worked on revisions of *Wise Blood*. She was personally dissatisfied with her work; in a letter to her friends Sally and Robert Fitzgerald, O'Connor wrote humorously of her feelings about her first novel: "Enclosed is Opus Nauseous No. I. I had to read it over after it came from the typist's and that was like spending the day eating a horse blanket. My mother said she wanted to read it again so she went off with it and I found her a half hour later on page 9 and sound asleep."[66]

Despite her misgivings about the suitability of her novel, O'Connor sent *Wise Blood* to Harcourt Brace in October 1951. After a round of minor revisions, the novel was published on May 15, 1952. The reviews were lukewarm, and southerners in general—and Milledgeville residents in particular—resented the book. Her friend and confidant Sally Fitzgerald writes of the reactions to the book:

> Southerners disliked it for what they saw as mockery of themselves and of Protestantism, and in her own locale [Milledgeville] it was regarded as a shockingly immoral book. . . . Northerners, too, including critics, though professing themselves not to be surprised by anything that happened in the South, found it too strong for their blood, and they, too, almost uniformly misunderstood it.[67]

Not only was the book not particularly well reviewed, but it also did not sell very well to the general public. O'Connor took the book's commercial failure philosophically, writing in a letter to a friend and fellow writer, "My first book was about freaks, but from now on I'm going to write about folks."[68] And writing about these folks in short stories would make her famous.

A Good Man Is Hard to Find

The two years following the publication of *Wise Blood* were productive ones for O'Connor. She worked on a number of short stories, which were published in several different magazines. O'Connor had also begun work on another novel, which would eventually appear as *The Violent Bear It Away*. She also began planning a collection of her short fiction that would bear the title of the first story in the book, *A Good Man Is Hard to Find*.

While O'Connor was producing much new work, her writing was also gaining acceptance with the critics. Several stories of O'Connor's were nominated for the O. Henry Award, and one, "A Circle of Fire," won second place in that competition.

By November 1954 the first draft of *A Good Man Is Hard to Find* was finished. When the book was published just a little more than six months later, it not only received praise from the literary critics but was also popular with the reading pub-

Writer O. Henry, after whom the respected short story award was named.

lic. Other successes followed: One story, "The Life You Save May Be Your Own," was sold to a television producer for eight hundred dollars; the magazine *Partisan Review* bought her story "A View of the Woods"; and best of all, a third story, "Greenleaf," won first prize in the O. Henry awards.

Making a Home in Georgia

O'Connor had hoped that her illness would improve so that she could eventually return to Connecticut, where she had been living before she fell ill. However, she finally realized that she would have to stay in Georgia, near people who could help her: her mother and Dr. Merrill, whose treatments were keeping her alive.

Unwilling to let her illness destroy her career, O'Connor turned her limitation into one of her strengths. The people who came to visit her in Milledgeville became the basis for the characters in her stories. In the words of Sally Fitzgerald, "She listened to and observed them carefully, spinning off wild and wonderful inventions from what she saw and heard, as she understood it in the light of what she knew and believed."[69] O'Connor was following the rule that is the key to success for many writers: One should write what one knows.

Physical Setbacks

O'Connor's professional successes, unfortunately, were matched by physical setbacks. The cortisone treatments that were controlling her lupus caused a deterioration of tissue in her hips, and she experienced intense pain that forced her to walk with a cane and later with crutches. In spite of needing care from her mother and her physician, O'Connor was able to make limited trips away from Milledgeville, addressing such groups as the Macon, Georgia, Writers' Club and the Macon Women's Club.

Meanwhile, O'Connor had continued working on her second novel. In the middle of 1955, she signed a contract with Harcourt Brace for its publication. The agreement gave her five years to complete work on the book, but even better, it called for the publisher to give her an advance of $1,250, which was considered a generous amount of money at the time.

The Violent Bear It Away

O'Connor's second novel was published as scheduled in 1960. However, because her contract with Harcourt Brace had contained a clause allowing her to be released if her editor resigned, the book was published by Farrar, Strauss, and Cudahy, where her old editor, Robert Giroux, was now working. Like most of her works, this book reflects her Christian beliefs, even though the characters and events in the novel often appear grotesque. Sally Fitzgerald writes of this work,

> The underlying premise of the whole [novel], however, is the author's belief, reflected in the old man [the character Mason Tarwater], that baptism in Christ is a matter of life and death. Of the fearsome events in this novel, [O'Connor] wrote, "I don't set out to be more drastic, but this happens automatically. If I write a novel in which the central action is a baptism, I know that for the larger percentage of my readers, baptism is a meaningless rite; therefore I have to embue this action with an awe and terror which will suggest its awful mystery. I have to distort the

O'Connor added awe and terror to her description of baptism (pictured) so that her readers could comprehend the importance of the rite.

look of the thing in order to represent as I see them both the mystery and the fact.[70]

The reviews of *The Violent Bear It Away* were mixed, but O'Connor took even the negative ones with characteristic good humor. In a letter to her friend Elizabeth Bishop, she wrote,

> My book has received considerable attention, most all of it simple-minded—a revolting review in *Time*, worse from Orville Prescott [a book reviewer], the usual snide paragraph in the *New Yorker*, & some very funny items from newspapers. The funniest to date was in the Savannah paper. . . . It was highly favorable, called the hero "Tarbutton" throughout and said he was nine years old [instead of fourteen].[71]

A Rapid Decline

The four years following the publication of *The Violent Bear It Away* continued to be productive. O'Connor worked on short stories, including "Everything That Rises Must Converge," which would be the title work of a new collection. But her health was now declining dramatically. Tests confirmed that her hips as well as her jaw were deteriorating due to the treatments that she relied on to control her lupus. The pain in her hips increased to the point that she proposed undergoing surgery to implant artificial joints. Her physician, however, advised against the operation, fearing that it would bring on a renewed attack of lupus.

By late summer 1963, O'Connor was suffering from anemia and tests eventually revealed that she had a fibroid tumor. Surgery was the only answer to this latest problem, and it was scheduled in spite of the high risk of causing a new attack of lupus. The surgery was successful, and by early March she was home, after having been treated for a kidney infection associated with the surgery.

The worst fears of her doctors were confirmed when the surgery and the postoperative infections reignited the lupus. Too weak to continue working on the stories she intended to include in *Everything That Rises Must Converge*, O'Connor instructed her editor to use the stories as they had appeared previously in magazines. But with great effort she completed two final stories for the collection.

O'Connor hoped to continue working, and she even had plans for yet another novel, although she never got beyond the opening chapter. Frustrated by her declining health, she wrote to a friend, "I've been writing for eighteen years and I've reached the point where I can't do again what I know I can do well, and the larger things I need to do now, I doubt my capacity for doing."[72]

The end came peacefully for O'Connor. On August 2, 1964, she slipped into a coma. Early in the morning of August 3, she died of kidney failure. She was buried next to her father in Memory Hill Cemetery in Milledgeville.

Had Flannery O'Connor lived on, she would almost certainly have continued writing. The generations of readers who have come since continue to be captivated by her sense of humor and by the often bizarre but always memorable characters she created.

CHAPTER 7

Toni Morrison: Witnessing Through Language

Although slavery was officially outlawed in the United States in 1865, African Americans continued to endure a confused status. Freed from slavery but not from the bonds of racial prejudice, blacks struggled not just for basic civil rights but also to define what, exactly, it meant to be African American. Through her writing, Toni Morrison eloquently uses language to portray the difficulties that African Americans have endured. In her words, "My attempt, although I never say any of this, until I'm done, is to deal with something that is nagging me, but, when I think about it in a large sense, I use the phrase 'bear witness' to explain what my work is for."[73]

Toni Morrison uses language to describe the difficulties that blacks have endured.

A Region From Which to Escape

Toni Morrison was born Chloe Anthony Wofford on February 18, 1931, in the gritty industrial city of Lorain, Ohio. The second of four children, Chloe had an older sister and two younger brothers. Her father, George Wofford, was a welder who worked in a shipyard. Chloe's mother, Rahmah, kept house for her family, at least during Chloe's childhood.

Both George Wofford and his wife had grown up in the South. George, in particular, had witnessed some of the terrible atrocities that white racists visited on blacks. Both had believed that leaving the South was a necessity. One scholar who has studied Toni Morrison's works says of her family's motivations for moving north, "Since [Chloe's parents] happened to be black, they thought of the South not as home but as a region from which they had escaped."[74]

Little Chloe's maternal grandparents had been sharecroppers, but they had always believed that education was the key to a better life. They passed this value along to Rahmah, who in turn instilled this same value in Chloe. In addition to valuing education, the Wofford family valued music. Chloe's mother liked to sing,

African American sharecroppers work in the fields picking cotton. Morrison's grandparents were sharecroppers who believed that a better life could be attained through education.

and her maternal grandfather, who also lived with the family, had once been a professional violinist. As scholar Karen Carmean tells it, "This was a household which also encouraged Morrison's imagination to grow, especially in the vein of black culture."[75] Chloe particularly admired her grandfather, John Solomon Willis, and he would eventually be immortalized in the title of one of her novels.

"We Were Intimate with the Supernatural"

In addition to the music that surrounded them, Chloe and her three siblings enjoyed the ghost stories their parents would share with them. Morrison later said in an interview, "We were intimate with the supernatural."[76]

There were less-positive influences in the household, however. Because of the abuses George Wofford had seen while growing up in the South, he was deeply distrustful of whites and their motivations. Later Morrison would say of her father, "As a child in Georgia, he received shocking impressions of adult white people, and for the rest of his life felt he was justified in despising all whites, and that they were not justified in despising him."[77]

Although Chloe rejected her father's outright hatred of white people, Wofford's contempt for whites inevitably affected his daughter. Of her father's influence on her thinking, Morrison would later say, "Thinking on it now I suppose I was backward, but I never longed for social integration with white people. . . . I was prey to the racism of my early years in Lorain where the only truly interesting people to me were the black people."[78]

A Precocious Child

Chloe's mother's influence was more positive than her father's was. Rahmah Wofford, who liked to read and was a member of a book club, instilled in Chloe a love of books. Given Rahmah's influence, perhaps it is not surprising that young Chloe proved to be a precocious child. By the time she entered the first grade in Lorain, she was the only child—white or black—who could read.

In addition to keeping on top of her schoolwork, Chloe had to help out around the house, and because money was always tight, she took a job cleaning house for a white family. The work was hard, and Chloe felt that the white housewife was mean to her. Chloe's father, however, reminded her that what these white people said or thought of her was of no importance—what counted was what she thought of herself.

Chloe Wofford's talent and intelligence kept her at or near the top of her class throughout her school years in Lorain, and in 1949 she graduated with honors from her high school.

During her years in school, Chloe had remained an avid reader, reading works by such writers as Jane Austen, Gustav Flaubert, and some of the great Russian novelists of the previous century, such as Tolstoy and Dostoyevsky. Later she would say, "These books were not written for a little black girl in Lorain, Ohio, but they were so magnificently done that I got them anyway."[79]

What fascinated Chloe, she recalled, was how these writers spoke directly about the cultures in which they had grown up. Later, she would speak of the influence these writers had on her own work: "When I wrote my first novel years later, I wanted to capture that same specificity about the nature and feeling of the culture *I* grew up in."[80]

On to College

With such obvious ability as a student, it is not surprising that Chloe's parents encouraged her to attend college, and she chose Howard University, an institution that had originally been founded as a black university and continued to attract a large black student body. To pay for his daughter's education, George Wofford took two extra jobs in addition to his job in the shipyard.

Being such a dedicated reader, it is also not surprising that she chose to major in literature. Toni Wofford (as she now referred to herself) also immersed herself in theater, joining the drama club called the Howard Unity Players. Ironically, despite its origins as an institution founded to provide advanced educational opportunities to blacks, Wofford found that black culture and consciousness were not a part of life at Howard. For example, when she proposed writing a term paper on black characters in Shakespeare's plays, her professor flatly rejected the idea, saying simply that such a topic was inappropriate.

A Taste for Scholarship

Wofford showed that she had a taste for scholarship when she went on to Cornell University for graduate work after graduating from Howard in 1953. She had decided to teach English at the college level, and after earning her master's degree in English in 1955, Wofford joined the faculty at Texas Southern University in Houston.

Wofford did not stay long at Texas Southern, however. When the chance came to take a faculty position at her undergraduate alma mater, she jumped at the opportunity. Back at Howard, Wofford settled into teaching general composition and literature.

Unfulfilled

Wofford's life was busy, and she was prospering professionally. Yet, she felt somehow unfulfilled. She needed to be doing something more with her talents, and that something was writing. To help herself achieve this goal, Wofford began attending meetings of a group of other writers and poets. Participants would share what they had written with members of the group, who would offer their critiques and suggestions.

Wofford began by sharing material she had produced while still in high school, but eventually she brought in a more recent attempt,

A pillar stands outside the Founders Library at Howard University, the school from which Morrison graduated in 1953.

a short story about a little black girl who wanted to have blue eyes. Wofford would later expand this story into her first novel, *The Bluest Eye*.

Besides taking the initial steps toward a career as a writer, Wofford had made other changes to her life. Just a year after her return to Howard, she met Harold Morrison, an architect from Jamaica. The two married in 1958, when Wofford was twenty-seven years old. The marriage was not destined to last, however, and the Morrisons divorced after seven years. Toni Morrison was single again, but she now had a preschool-age son, and was expecting another baby, conceived prior to her divorce.

A New Career

Following the breakup of her marriage, Morrison resigned from her faculty position. She briefly returned to her family home in Ohio, but she eventually settled in Syracuse, New York, where she landed a job as an editor with the I. W. Singer Publishing House, a subsidiary of Random House.

Although she began her new career as a textbook editor, it was not long before she made the jump to publishing trade books—that is, novels and nonfiction books for general readers. Again, Morrison showed that she had talent, and she was soon promoted to senior editor.

Morrison raised her two sons while working as a novelist and full-time editor.

Like "a Dirty Habit"

Morrison's job as senior editor at Random House kept her busy, but she still made time to work on her own fiction. She recalls, "I wrote like someone with a dirty habit. Secretly, compulsively, slyly."[81] She was working on a novel based on the short story she had shown to the writing group while she was still teaching at Howard.

Morrison had shown her story to Alan Rancler, an editor at another publisher, Macmillan. Rancler encouraged her to expand the short story into a novel. Morrison tried to convince herself that this was just something she was doing for her own satisfaction—that it made no difference whether a publisher was interested in it. Yet, she could not help being disappointed when she was faced with a decided lack of interest from the publishers to whom she showed the manuscript. But then Rancler, who by then had moved to the publisher Holt, Rinehart, and Winston, agreed to publish the novel. Entitled *The Bluest Eye*, the novel would change Toni Morrison's life.

Morrison's purpose in writing *The Bluest Eye* was to show how all individuals can learn to survive, despite the adversities that befall them. In Morrison's words, "I suppose *The Bluest Eye* is about one's dependency on the world for identification, self-value, feelings of worth."[82]

Critics praised *The Bluest Eye*, but most meaningful to Morrison was the fact that she had at last found fulfillment. In her recollection, "Writing became a way to become coherent in the world."[83]

Balancing a demanding full-time job against the requirements of raising two sons alone was hard; adding a second career as a novelist would simply be beyond many people. Random House helped Morrison by allowing her to work at home, but still she was swamped. However, Morrison rejected the idea that women must choose between a professional career and homemaking, observing that black women had been managing to do what seemed impossible for hundreds of years: "We're managing households and other people's children and two jobs and listening to everybody and at the same time creating, singing, holding, bearing, transferring the culture for generations. We've been walking on water for four hundred years."[84]

A Major New Force in Literature

By the time her first novel was published, Toni Morrison was already working on her second, entitled *Sula*. Upon its publication in 1974, Morrison's career as a novelist took off. She received the

Morrison believes that African Americans must gain knowledge of their past and apply it to the present, thus "reintroducing themselves."

great honor of having this novel nominated for the prestigious National Book Award, which was just one indication that Morrison was a major new force in literature. *Sula* also marked a change in Morrison's own thinking: Blacks needed to be conscious of their own culture, but they also needed to struggle for personal self-realization. In Morrison's words, "What we [blacks] have to do is reintroduce ourselves to ourselves. We have to know the past so that we can use it for now."[85]

Morrison's next novel was even better received than *Sula. Song of Solomon*, published in 1977, won the Critics' Circle Award for fiction and the American Academy and Institute of Arts and Letters Award. In addition, the novel became the first by an African American woman to be selected by the Book-of-the-Month Club, which ensured that it would enjoy healthy sales to the reading public.

A Difficult Novel

Morrison kept setting a higher and higher standard for her own work. Her fourth novel, *Tar Baby*, was particularly ambitious; she filled the book with numerous themes and literary allusions. The result was a novel that critics have come to love but the reading public has trouble digesting. Scholar Karen Carmean phrases the problem with the book this way: "Morrison challenged herself so consciously in this novel to do her best that she wound up with one of those novels that people tend to call 'difficult.' In other words, the meaning of the story wasn't plainly on the surface."[86]

As Morrison's reputation as a novelist grew, more honors rolled in. She was offered prestigious teaching posts, such the Albert Schweitzer Professor of Humanities at the State University of New York at Albany. But even greater honors awaited. When Morrison's fifth novel, *Beloved*, was published in 1987, it won the Pulitzer Prize for fiction. *Beloved* chronicles the story of escaped slave, Margaret Garner, who, rather than allow her four children to return to slavery, tries to kill them. Morrison's stated purpose in writing this novel was "to show the malevolence of the institution itself through a family that was devastated by slavery."[87]

The popularity of *Beloved* surprised even Morrison. In fact, because the novel's themes of slavery and the violence that accompanied it were ugly and difficult to dwell on, Morrison believed that she was running the risk of writing something that nobody would want to read.

The praise that *Beloved* gained for Morrison led Princeton University, one of the most highly respected institutions in the world, to offer her the Robert F. Goheen Professorship in the Humanities. This was, of course, an honor, but it paled in comparison to the one that awaited.

A Landmark Accomplishment

With the publication of *Beloved*, Morrison set out to write the second novel in what she planned to be a trilogy. The new novel, *Jazz*, is not, however, a sequel to *Beloved* in the sense of sharing any characters or settings. But as Carmean writes, "In terms of chronology, *Jazz* does pick up roughly where *Beloved* left off and continues the greater story Morrison wishes to tell in her trilogy in progress, the story of her people passing through their American experience, from the days of slavery up to the present."[88]

In 1993, just a year after the publication of *Jazz*, Morrison received her greatest honor: the Nobel Prize for literature. In awarding her the prize, the Swedish Academy noted that Toni Morrison, "in novels characterized by visionary force and poetic import, gives life to an essential aspect of American reality."[89] Morrison was only the eighth woman to win the prize, and she was the first black woman to do so.

Other honors have come Morrison's way since she won the Nobel Prize. For example, in 1995 she was presented with the Matrix Award by the organization Women in Communications. This award is presented each year to women who have made major contributions in the field of communications, and

Morrison was recognized in the book category. Also in 1995, Howard University awarded her an honorary doctorate

Continuing to Witness

Toni Morrison continues to write, bearing witness to the struggles of African Americans as they come to terms with their history and overcome the legacy of oppression that made up such a large portion of that history. Her latest novel, *Paradise*, which tells how the residents of a tiny all-black hamlet attack a nearby community of women, was published in 1997.

When she undertakes a new project, Morrison refuses to be hurried. She thoroughly thinks over her subject matter and style. Then—sometimes—she will write out a brief overview of what her book will be about, although she never works from an outline. Morrison says that she never rushes to begin the actual writing: "I may think about it for two years before I even get down to shaping a sentence on a page."[90]

Morrison's career as a writer took a different turn in 1999, when she collaborated with her adult son, Slade Morrison, to publish a book for young children entitled *The Big Box*. Beautifully illustrated, this brief book tells the story of three children who yearn merely to be themselves.

Toni Morrison receives the Nobel Prize for literature from Sweden's King Carl Gustaf XVI. Morrison is the first African American woman to receive the award.

Morrison's life is a full one, and she is constantly busy with various speaking engagements, as well as with her teaching responsibilities at Princeton. She says that her work is enjoyable and takes the place of vacations. Where Morrison's next "vacation" will take her is only a matter of conjecture, but what is unquestionable is that the work she produces will be read and talked about well into the twenty-first century.

NOTES

Chapter 1: A New Literature for a New Society

1. Paul S. Boyer et al., *The Enduring Vision*. 2nd ed. Boston: DC Heath, 1995, p. 471.

2. Boyer, *The Enduring Vision*, p. 470.

3. Nina Baym, ed., *The Norton Anthology of American Literature*, vol. 1, 5th ed. New York: W. W. Norton, 1998, p. 911.

4. Baym, *The Norton Anthology of American Literature*, p. 911.

5. Baym, *The Norton Anthology of American Literature*, p. 919.

6. Boyer, *The Enduring Vision*, p. 569.

7. Quoted in Boyer, *The Enduring Vision*, p. 570.

8. Baym, *The Norton Anthology of American Literature*, p. 1776.

9. Boyer, *The Enduring Vision*, p. 648.

10. Baym, *The Norton Anthology of American Literature*, p. 1777.

11. Baym, *The Norton Anthology of American Literature*, p. 1779.

12. Boyer, *The Enduring Vision*, p. 668.

13. Quoted in Boyer, *The Enduring Vision*, p. 678.

Chapter 2: John Steinbeck: A Voice for the Dispossessed

14. Quoted in Jay Parini, *John Steinbeck: A Biography*. New York: Henry Holt, 1995, pp. 11–12.

15. Parini, *John Steinbeck*, p. 24.

16. Quoted in Parini, *John Steinbeck*, p. 53.

17. Quoted in Parini, *John Steinbeck*, p. 99.

18. Quoted in Parini, *John Steinbeck*, pp. 176–77.

19. Quoted in Parini, *John Steinbeck*, p. 271.

20. Quoted in Parini, *John Steinbeck*, p. 347.

21. Quoted in Parini, *John Steinbeck*, p. 383.

22. Quoted in Parini, *John Steinbeck*, p. 431.

23. Quoted in Parini, *John Steinbeck*, p. 447.

Chapter 3: Ernest Hemingway: The Solitary Hero

24. Quoted in Carlos Baker, *Ernest Hemingway: A Life Story*. New York: Charles Scribner's Sons, 1969, p. 5.

25. Baker, *Ernest Hemingway*, p. 9.

26. Quoted in Baker, *Ernest Hemingway*, p. 84.

27. Quoted in Baker, *Ernest Hemingway*, p. 178.

28. Anthony Burgess, *Ernest Hemingway*. London: Thames and Hudson, 1978, p. 57.

29. Burgess, *Ernest Hemingway*, pp. 100–101.

30. Richard B. Lyttle, *Ernest Hemingway: The Life and the Legend*. New York: Atheneum, 1992, pp. 176–77.

31. Burgess, *Ernest Hemingway*, p. 106.

Chapter 4: William Faulkner: A Son of the South
32. Stephen B. Oates, *William Faulkner: The Man and the Artist, a Biography*. New York: Harper & Row, 1987, p. 6.

33. Quoted in Oates, *William Faulkner*, p. 13.

34. Oates, *William Faulkner*, p. 17.

35. Quoted in Oates, *William Faulkner*, p. 31.

36. Quoted in Oates, *William Faulkner*, p. 38.

37. Oates, *William Faulkner*, p. 75.

38. Oates, *William Faulkner*, p. 81.

39. Oates, *William Faulkner*, p. 85.

40. Oates, *William Faulkner*, p. 87.

41. Quoted in Oates, *William Faulkner*, p. 163.

42. Quoted in Oates, *William Faulkner*, p. 196.

43. Quoted in Oates, *William Faulkner*, p. 245.

44. Quoted in Oates, *William Faulkner*, pp. 249–50.

45. Quoted in Oates, *William Faulkner*, p. 322.

Chapter 5: James Baldwin: Victory over Silence
46. James Campbell, *Talking at the Gates: A Life of James Baldwin*. New York: Viking Penguin, 1991, p. 4.

47. Quoted in Campbell, *Talking at the Gates*, p. 13.

48. Quoted in Campbell, *Talking at the Gates*, p. 21.

49. Campbell, *Talking at the Gates*, p. 33.

50. W. J. Weatherby, *James Baldwin: Artist on Fire*. New York: Donald L. Fine, 1989, p. 63.

51. Quoted in Weatherby, *James Baldwin*, p. 74.

52. Campbell, *Talking at the Gates*, p. 61.

53. Quoted in Campbell, *Talking at the Gates*, p. 84.

54. Campbell, *Talking at the Gates*, p. 110.

55. Quoted in Campbell, *Talking at the Gates*, p. 121.

56. Quoted in Campbell, *Talking at the Gates*, p. 124.

57. Weatherby, *James Baldwin*, p. 198.

58. Quoted in Weatherby, *James Baldwin*, pp. 222–23.

59. Quoted in Campbell, *Talking at the Gates*, p. 200.

60. Campbell, *Talking at the Gates*, p. 250.

61. Quoted in Campbell, *Talking at the Gates*, p. 282.

Chapter 6: Flannery O'Connor: The Voice of Southern Gothic

62. Flannery O'Connor, *Collected Works*. New York: Literary Classics of the United States, 1988, p. 805.

63. O'Connor, *Collected Works*, p. 879.

64. O'Connor, *Collected Works*, p. 880.

65. O'Connor, *Collected Works*, pp. 882–83.

66. O'Connor, *Collected Works*, p. 891.

67. Sally Fitzgerald, introduction to *Three by Flannery O'Connor*, by Flannery O'Connor. New York: Penguin, 1983, pp. xiv–xv.

68. Quoted in Fitzgerald, introduction to *Three by Flannery O'Connor*, p. xv.

69. Fitzgerald, introduction to *Three by Flannery O'Connor*, p. xviii.

70. Fitzgerald, introduction to *Three by Flannery O'Connor*, pp. xix–xx.

71. O'Connor, *Collected Works*, p. 1126.

72. Quoted in Fitzgerald, introduction to *Three by Flannery O'Connor*, p. xxii.

Chapter 7: Toni Morrison: Witnessing Through Language

73. Quoted in Karen Carmean, *Toni Morrison's World of Fiction*. Troy, NY: Whitson, 1993, p. 17.

74. Carmean, *Toni Morrison's World of Fiction*, p. 1.

75. Carmean, *Toni Morrison's World of Fiction*, p. 2.

76. Quoted in Wilfred D. Samuels and Clenora Hudson-Weems, *Toni Morrison*. Boston: Twayne, 1990, p. 4.

77. Quoted in Samuels and Hudson-Weems, *Toni Morrison*, p. 3.

78. Quoted in Linden Peach, *Toni Morrison*. New York: St. Martin's, 1995, p. 5.

79. Quoted in Carmean, *Toni Morrison's World of Fiction*, p. 3.

80. Quoted in Carmean, *Toni Morrison's World of Fiction*, p. 3.

81. Quoted in Carmean, *Toni Morrison's World of Fiction*, p. 4.

82. Quoted in Carmean, *Toni Morrison's World of Fiction*, p. 18.

83. Quoted in Samuels and Hudson-Weems, *Toni Morrison*, p. 7.

84. Quoted in Missy Dean Kubitschek, *Toni Morrison: A Critical Companion*. Westport, CT: Greenwood, 1998, p. 5.

85. Quoted in Samuels and Hudson-Weems, *Toni Morrison*, p. 7.

86. Carmean, *Toni Morrison's World of Fiction*, p. 63.

87. Quoted in Samuels and Hudson-Weems, *Toni Morrison*, p. 9.

88. Carmean, *Toni Morrison's World of Fiction*, p. 100.

89. Quoted in Toni Morrison, *The Nobel Lecture in Literature*. New York: Knopf, 1993, p. 5.

90. Quoted in Carmean, *Toni Morrison's World of Fiction*, p. 6.

FOR FURTHER READING

Susan Balee, *Flannery O'Connor: Literary Prophet of the South.* New York: Chelsea House, 1995. Portrays O'Connor's life and works, and provides historical details about the American South and how such events impacted O'Connor and her family.

Douglas Century, *Toni Morrison.* New York: Chelsea House, 1994. This biography not only gives details of Morrison's life but also discusses major themes and characters in her novels.

Barbara Cramer, *Toni Morrison: Nobel Prize–Winning Author.* Springfield, NJ: Enslow, 1996. Details Morrison's life and major works, includes information on plots, characters, and themes in her novels.

Tom Ito, *The Importance of John Steinbeck.* San Diego: Lucent Books, 1994. Provides insights into Steinbeck's life and his works. Places the author's life in the context of events in American history.

Katie de Koster, ed., *Readings on Ernest Hemingway.* San Diego: Greenhaven, 1997. Provides a brief overview of Hemingway's life, followed by essays by noted scholars on Hemingway's major works.

Paula Bryant Pratt, *The Importance of Ernest Hemingway.* San Diego: Lucent Books, 1999. Details Hemingway's life and works and includes many quotes from Hemingway himself.

Clarice Swisher, ed., *Readings on William Faulkner.* San Diego: Greenhaven, 1997. Provides a brief overview of Faulkner's life, followed by essays by noted scholars on Faulkner's major works.

James Tackach, *The Importance of James Baldwin.* San Diego: Lucent Books, 1997. Provides information on Baldwin and his works as well as details about the American civil rights movement and Baldwin's involvement in it.

WORKS CONSULTED

Carlos Baker, *Ernest Hemingway: A Life Story*. New York: Charles Scribner's Sons, 1969. A detailed biography of Hemingway by a noted scholar. Contains many photos taken over the course of Hemingway's life.

Nina Baym, ed., *The Northern Anthology of American Literature*. Vol. 1, 5th ed. New York: W. W. Norton, 1998. This widely studied collection of American literature, along with its companion first volume, provides excellent information about literary trends throughout American history, as well as brief biographical sketches of key American writers.

Paul S. Boyer et al., *The Enduring Vision*. 2nd ed. Boston: DC Heath, 1995. An excellent source of information about the social history of the United States.

Anthony Burgess, *Ernest Hemingway*. London: Thames and Hudson, 1978. A brief and somewhat scholarly treatment of Hemingway's life.

James Campbell, *Talking at the Gates: A Life of James Baldwin*. New York: Viking Penguin, 1991. A detailed examination of Baldwin's life and work. Contains excellent analyses of all of Baldwin's major works.

Karen Carmean, *Toni Morrison's World of Fiction*. Troy, NY: Whitson, 1993. A collection of essays on Morrison's major works; this volume features an introductory biographical sketch.

Missy Dean Kubitschek, *Toni Morrison: A Critical Companion*. Westport, CT: Greenwood, 1998. This scholarly work contains essays on Morrison's work plus an opening biographical sketch.

Richard B. Lyttle, *Ernest Hemingway: The Life and the Legend*. New York: Atheneum, 1992. An excellent biography of Hemingway. Includes photographs of the author taken over the course of his life.

Toni Morrison, *The Nobel Lecture in Literature*. New York: Knopf, 1993. A reprint of Morrison's speech upon accepting the 1993 Nobel Prize for literature.

Stephen B. Oates, *William Faulkner: The Man and the Artist, a Biography*. New York: Harper & Row, 1987. A detailed account of Faulkner's life; this volume also contains detailed summaries of Faulkner's major works.

Flannery O'Connor, *Collected Works*. New York: Literary Classics of the United States, 1988. This compilation of fiction, letters, and nonfiction prose of Flannery O'Connor is an invaluable resource for anyone studying her work and life. Contains a highly detailed chronology of O'Connor's life.

————, *Three by Flannery O'Connor*. New York: Penguin, 1983. This collection of three of O'Connor's works includes an introduction written by her longtime friend Sally Fitzgerald. Fitzgerald's insights and recollections of incidents in O'Connor's life are helpful in understanding this complex writer's perspectives.

Jay Parini, *John Steinbeck: A Biography*. New York: Henry Holt, 1995. A sympathetic but honest treatment of the author, his works, and his personal relationships.

Linden Peach, *Toni Morrison*. New York: St. Martin's, 1995. A scholar's look at Morrison's major works.

Wilfred D. Samuels and Clenora Hudson-Weems, *Toni Morrison*. Boston: Twayne, 1990. A critical analysis of Morrison's work; this volume also features biographical information.

W. J. Weatherby, *James Baldwin: Artist on Fire*. New York: Donald L. Fine, 1989. A sympathetic portrait of Baldwin that does an excellent job of placing the author's life in a historical context.

INDEX

Absalom, Absalom! (Faulkner), 56
African Americans
  cities and, 10, 12–14
  civil rights movement and, 16,
    19–20, 68–69
  Harlem Renaissance and, 13–14
  1920s and, 12
  as portrayed by
    Baldwin, 8–9, 66–67, 69,
     71–72
    Morrison, 9, 87, 92, 94, 95,
     96
  segregation and, 16
  World War II and, 15
Alfred A. Knopf (publisher), 54, 66
Amen Corner, The (Baldwin), 67
American Academy and Institute of
  Arts and Letters, 94
American Academy of Arts and
  Letters, 30, 58
American culture
  consumerism in, 15, 18, 32
  diversity of, 17, 18, 20
American dream, 15–16, 18
American Red Cross, 38
Ames, Elizabeth, 81
Anderson, Sherwood, 39, 50
Angelou, Maya, 73
Another Country (Baldwin), 71

baby boom generation, 18
Baker, Carlos
  on Hemingway's memories of
    father, 36
  on *The Winter of Our
    Discontent* (Steinbeck), 32
Baldwin, David (brother), 72–73
Baldwin, David (stepfather), 62, 63
Baldwin, James
  alcohol and, 72
  characteristics of, 68
  characters of, 8–9, 66–67, 69,
    71–72
  childhood of, 62
  civil rights movement and, 68–69
  death of, 73
  in Europe, 64–68
  on fame, 71

  family of, 61–62
  Great Depression and, 62
  health of, 72–73
  homosexuality of, 64, 67–68
  on importance of relationship
    with Delaney, 62
  as laborer, 63
  as literary critic, 64
  Morrison and, 73
  Muhammad and, 70
  plots of, 66
  racism and, 64, 69
  religion and, 62
  Robert F. Kennedy and, 71
  style of, 62
  themes of, 8–9, 66–67, 69, 71
  works of, 72
    Amen Corner, The, 67
    Another Country, 71
    Crying Holy, 63–64, 66
    essays
      "Down at the Cross,"
       70–71
      "Everybody's Protest
       Novel," 65
      "Letter from a Region of
       My Mind," 71
      "Stranger in the Village,"
       66–67
    Fire Next Time, The, 70, 71
    Giovanni's Room, 67
    Go Tell It on the Mountain,
     66, 67
    Just Above My Head, 72
    *Nobody Knows My Name:
     More Notes of a Native Son,*
     69
    No Name in the Street, 69
    Notes of a Native Son, 67
    reviews, 64
    *Tell Me How Long the Train's
     Been Gone,* 71–72
    unfinished
     No Papers for Muhammad,
     72
     Remember This House, 72
    Welcome House, The, 72
Ballou, Robert O., 27

PICTURE CREDITS

ABOUT THE AUTHOR

Elizabeth Meehan lives in San Diego and is Professor of English and Humanities at San Diego City College. She earned her bachelor's degree from the University of California, San Diego and her master's degree from Claremont Graduate School.